CONTEMPORARY

EDGE ON ENGLISH

ALL SPELLED OUT

B

Betsy Rubin

Project Editors
Deborah M. Newton Chocolate
David Caes

Published by Contemporary Books, Inc.
Two Prudential Plaza, Chicago, Illinois 60601-6790
Manufactured in the United States of America
International Standard Book Number: 0-8092-5200-7

Published simultaneously in Canada by
Fitzhenry & Whiteside
195 Allstate Parkway
Markham, Ontario L3R 4T8
Canada

Editorial
Julie Landau
Christine M. Benton

Editorial Director
Caren Van Slyke

Production Editor
Patricia Reid

Illustrator
Maxine Shore

Art Director
Georgene G. Sainati

Art & Production
Princess Louise El
Arvid Carlson
Lois Koehler

Cover Design
William Ewing

For Caroline and Mischa

CONTENTS

To the Instructor   **vi**

To the Student   **1**

CHAPTER 1

Try Your Hand at Spelling Skills   **3**

Letters, Sounds, Vowels, and Consonants   **4**

Short Vowel Sounds   **5**

WORD PARTS: Short Vowels and Suffixes   **7**

DICTIONARY SKILLS: Alphabetizing   **9**

WORDS FOR NOW: Filling Out a Job Application   **11**

CHAPTER 2

LONG VOWELS: Mop or Mope (VCe)   **14**

WORD PARTS: Suffixes on VCe Words (-S and -ED)   **17**

WORD PARTS: Suffixes on VCe Words (-ING)   **18**

LONG VOWEL SOUNDS: Sweet Dreams (VV)   **19**

WORD PARTS: More Suffixes with Long Vowels   **20**

WORD PARTS: Suffixes: Double Consonants   **21**

WORDS FOR NOW: Phone Messages   **23**

DICTIONARY SKILLS: Guide Words   **25**

CHAPTER 3

LONG VOWELS: Cheers! A Toast! (ō)   **27**

LONG VOWELS: A Close Shave (ā)   **32**

DICTIONARY SKILLS: Looking up a Spelling   **35**

LONG VOWELS: A Fight! A Fight! (ī)   **37**

WORD PARTS: Suffixes after *Y*   **40**

WORDS FOR NOW: Numbers   **42**

LONG VOWELS: Am I Blue? (ū or o͞o)   **45**

LONG VOWELS: Where's the Beef? (ē)   **49**

LONG VOWELS: Feel the Chill (ē, ĭ)   **54**

WORDS FOR NOW: Food Words   **56**

CHAPTER 4

CONSONANT COMBOS: Snatch a Smooch (CH)   58
CONSONANT COMBOS: Pass the Butter Please (SS, SE)   60
DICTIONARY SKILLS: Finding the Right Spelling   62
WORD PARTS: Plurals   64
CONSONANT COMBOS: Three Months (TH)   69
CONSONANT COMBOS: She'll Be Here Shortly (SH)   71
WORDS FOR NOW: Days and Months   74
WORDS TO USE: Possessive Nouns   76

CHAPTER 5

WAYS TO SPELL A SOUND: Kind to Call (K)   79
WAYS TO SPELL A SOUND: Grease on the Dress (S)   83
WORDS FOR NOW: Letter to a Teacher   87
WAYS TO SPELL A SOUND: Junior Has Germs (J)   90
WAYS TO SPELL A SOUND: I Guess He's Guilty (G)   93
WORDS TO USE: Prepositions   95
WAYS TO SPELL A SOUND: Where's the Wine? (W)   97
DICTIONARY SKILLS: Trial and Error   99
DICTIONARY SKILLS: Review   101
WORD PARTS: Suffix Review   103
REVIEW: Final Words   105
APPENDIX: Symbols Used in This Book   110

ANSWER KEY   111

To the Instructor

If good spelling is important to the overall effectiveness of writing, then how do students who are lacking in both areas develop the skills necessary to communicate clearly? What approaches can be taken to motivate a student to want to learn how to spell correctly? One way is to help students to realize that good writing and spelling can help them to attain their occupational and educational goals.

In order to become a strong speller, a student must learn to combine skills of observation, application, and memorization. Spelling patterns that govern much of what must be learned here can actually help students recognize the spelling patterns of other words. But because all words do not follow rules, some of the harder-to-spell words will simply have to be memorized. A good speller will also learn to rely upon the dictionary for help in building spelling skills. In addition to learning spelling and dictionary skills, students can practice what they have learned through writing exercises that test their spelling ability.

SCOPE OF BOOK

Aimed at both teens and adults who are acquiring basic spelling skills, **All Spelled Out B** emphasizes one-syllable words, as well as longer words that are useful to the student in everyday applications.

Skill-building activities shape a significant portion of the book since the chief objective is the acquisition of skills that can be applied to spell many words correctly. The word lists included in each lesson are to be regarded as resources, and students should not be required to memorize any word lists from this book unless they decide to do so on their own.

ORGANIZATION

All Spelled Out B focuses on the long vowel spelling patterns and the consonant patterns found in words. Homophones, or "Words That Sound Alike," as well as grammatical endings -s, -ed, -ing, are taught in developmental lessons. "Words to Use" is a feature that focuses on common words for everyday usage, such as possessive nouns and prepositions. And in "Words for Now," word lists for practical life skills tasks are introduced. Finally, dictionary skills foster students' spelling independence.

LESSONS

Students discover "Insights" into spelling patterns by studying a sample list of words or an introductory sentence to the lesson. "Words to Learn" are words that do not follow the spelling rules. The two are combined within the lesson's exercises to enhance the students' ability either to apply a spelling pattern or to recognize a word that does not follow a pattern.

Word games, including crossword puzzles, and word grids, have been devised to help the students have fun while increasing their powers of observation and generalization. Practice with writing sentences and paragraphs as well as proofreading exercises help sharpen the students' spelling abilities.

HOW TO USE THIS BOOK

All Spelled Out B is designed for use either within or outside the classroom setting. Within the classroom, the instructor should walk the students through the "Insight" exercises. However, lessons have been designed so that students can work through these exercises on their own.

Spelling notebooks should be used by the students for especially hard-to-spell words or for words that individual students wish to learn. You can reinforce spelling skills acquisition by prompting students to develop their own spelling program. A great motivation in learning to spell is for students to identify and practice words that are important to them.

Encourage students to use their dictionaries in classroom writing assignments in order to find words whose spellings they are uncertain of. Distribute books and newspapers to allow students to discover new words that contain spelling patterns they have already learned.

Proofreading and dictation exercises should be used by the instructor as supplements designed to combine spelling with writing, sentence meaning, and grammar. Be careful to use only those words or spelling patterns that have been studied by the student. Quizzes for determining proofreading ability can be designed based on the proofreading exercises in this book.

To provide a change of pace, as well as both practice and a spelling challenge, make use of such commercial word games as Boggle, Scrabble, and Spill 'n' Spell. Here is another simple game: write a long word on the blackboard and have the students find as many short words within that word as possible. And don't forget the old spelling standbys: hangman and spelling bees.

RELATED SKILLS

The key to good spelling is a good understanding of grammar, vocabulary, and pronunciation. Spelling rules seem to fall apart when a student does not have a grasp of correct English usage. For instance, if a student does not know that the preposition *to*, is needed in the sentence "I went to the store," a lesson contrasting *to*, *too*, and *two*, will make little or no sense at all. Allow the student to learn the spelling of words that are already a part of his or her speaking vocabulary.

Regional speech patterns and ethnicity play a large part in acceptable pronunciation of the English language. Wherever a student's pronunciation interferes with spelling a word, the instructor should make a note of it but should not intimate that the pronunciation is incorrect. For example, many people pronounce the word *ask* as *ax*. The instructor can help the student hear the letters *s* and *k* that are necessary for the correct spelling of the word. However, the instructor should not attempt to have the students change their system of pronunciation.

SYMBOLS AND RULES

The explanations, rules, and symbols used in **All Spelled Out B** have been selected with the student in mind. The book presents only those spelling patterns that generate enough words to make learning the pattern worthwhile. The sounds and spelling patterns are represented by symbols or notations that are meant to be as simple and as clear as possible.

DOS AND DON'TS

To help your students become good spellers, keep these suggestions in mind:

1. Frequently emphasize the role of correct spelling in making a good impression in the students' education, social life, and economic future.
2. Encourage students to observe words and patterns in words whenever they read and write.
3. Acknowledge that English spelling can be tricky, but stress that it can be learned.
4. Reinforce the grammar and vocabulary skills that are related to spelling skills.
5. Urge students to take the responsibility for deciding which words they want to learn to spell, and encourage them to learn the spelling of these words on their own.
6. Show students that while spelling can be difficult, it can also be fun.

WHY IS SPELLING IMPORTANT?

Imagine that you are recruiting students for your training program. Two students enter your office. You ask each of them to fill out an application to the program and you read both applications.

Name **Jody Sawyer**

Address **1127 Wisconsin Ave., River Grove, IL**

Phone **555-3651**

Which program are you interested in?

Computer operator

Why are you interested?

I would like to make more money.

List your previous jobs.

Dishwasher, shipping clerk

Name **Chris Johnson**

Address **1826 Wikon Avanue, River Grove, Il**

Phone **555-0715**

Which program are you interested in?

Computor oprator

Why are you interested?

I think I would injoy working wit computors.

List your previous jobs.

Kar mekanic, gastation atendent

Which makes the better impression? The second is hard to read. The misspellings interfere with the reader's making sense out of the application.

As the recruiter, which candidate would you pick? Does the applicant's spelling make a difference?

When it comes to making a good impression, correct spelling is as important as wearing the right clothes. Good spelling can sometimes mean the difference between getting into a program or not. As a matter of fact, whenever you fill out a form or write a letter or note, your spelling tells others something about you. Can you think of any other times when spelling might be important?

SPELLING SENSE AND HOW TO GET IT

"But I've never been able to spell!" you say. Wait. Stop thinking that you can't spell. You **can** learn how, and this book will help you.

Almost everyone has trouble with spelling at one time or another. Is it "prefer" or "perfer"? "Libary" or "library"? "Article" or "artical"?

Our spelling has a very long history. Words have come to us from different languages, and our pronunciation has changed over the years. English spelling reflects this word history.

Our spelling system is not completely crazy. There **are** rules. This book will help you learn some of these rules so that you'll be able to spell better. This book will also help you with the spellings of some tricky words that you might need to use. You will also find words for special needs, such as applying for a job or writing a letter.

Is this just a book of vocabulary lists? No. You won't need to memorize long lists of words. You already have a large vocabulary. What you need are the skills to spell the words you already know! You need spelling sense.

One secret to becoming a good speller is to use your powers of observation. You have to **look** at words. Many of the games and exercises in this book will help you do this. Another secret is knowing how to use a dictionary to find words you don't know how to spell. The dictionary exercises in this book will help you build these skills.

This brings us to the materials you will need. Buy a pocket dictionary and keep it handy. (Your instructor can suggest a good one.) You will also want to get a notebook in which to write sample words, tricky words, and other pieces of writing. You can use your notebook to work on your own spelling program and focus on the words you need to know.

With some work, and a little fun, you can build your spelling sense. Good luck!

THE ANSWER KEY CAN BE FOUND IN THE BACK OF THE BOOK, BEGINNING ON PAGE 111.

CHAPTER 1

Goals

SOUNDS TO SPELL: Letters, Sounds, Vowels, and Consonants
SHORT VOWEL SOUNDS: VC and VCC Patterns
Short Vowels and Suffixes
DICTIONARY SKILLS: Alphabetizing
WORDS FOR NOW: Job Application

Try Your Hand at Spelling Skills

SIGHT AND SOUND

Say each word out loud as you look at it. Notice that some of the words rhyme (sound alike).

SAMPLE WORDS

List A	List B
smell	sip
lack	cot
hip	bell
dot	rack

Work on your powers of observation! Look at each word carefully as you say it. Say each letter out loud. Then look away and write the word in your notebook. Now check back, to see if you wrote it correctly. Use this simple exercise—**Say-Copy-Check**—whenever you want to learn the spelling of a word.

Look for words with the same spelling patterns. Write the rhyming word from List B next to each word below.

smell __**bell**_____

lack _____

hip _____

dot _____

Now go back to each word and think of words with the same spelling pattern. Write them on the lines above.

Example: smell **bell, fell**_____

BEING A GOOD SPELLER MEANS LOOKING AT WORDS
CAREFULLY. USE THE **SAY-COPY-CHECK** EXERCISE
WITH NEW OR HARD WORDS. ALWAYS TRY TO
FIND PATTERNS IN WORDS.

Letters, Sounds, Vowels, and Consonants

VOWEL AND CONSONANT LETTERS

There are two kinds of letters in the alphabet. The letters *a, e, i, o,* and *u* are called **vowels.** All other letters (*b, c, d, f,* and so on) are called **consonants.** (*Y* can be either a vowel or a consonant, but you'll learn more about *y* later.) To learn to spell well, you must be able to distinguish consonants from vowels.

In the words below, circle all the vowels and underline all the consonants. The first one has been done for you.

<u>c</u>(o)<u>ns</u>(o)<u>n</u>(a)<u>nts</u>   circle   vowels   more   letters

LETTERS AND SOUNDS

By now you've learned that some letters are vowels and some letters are consonants.

What are the vowel letters? Write them here: __a,_____

Next, look at the words below. What one vowel letter do you see in all the words? _____

hand   tall   late   father

Say each word out loud and hear how the letter *a* sounds different in each word. You can see that one letter can have more than one **sound.** In fact, there are five vowel letters but many more vowel sounds! You'll soon learn about the spelling patterns that show each sound.

This book will use symbols to show which **sound** is being talked about. Each symbol has a name. For example, ă is the symbol for the "short A" sound in *hand;* ā is the symbol for the "long A" sound in *late.*

Short Vowel Sounds

In the next section of this book, you will be focusing on long vowel sounds. Before you work with long vowel sounds, it would be helpful to review the short vowel sounds.

Focus on the short vowel sounds.

Say these words: **pat   man.**   Say the vowel sound you hear in each word. The sound that you say in *pat* and *man* is called short *a*. We use the symbol *ă* to show this sound.

Say these words: **pet   fed.**   Say the vowel sound you hear in each word. The sound that you say in *pet* and *fed* is called short *e*. We use the symbol *ě* to show this sound.

Say these words: **hit   lid.**   Say the vowel sound you hear in each word. The sound that you say in *hit* and *lid* is called short *i*. Use the symbol *ĭ* to show this sound.

Say these words: **hop   rob.**   Say the vowel sound you hear in each word. The sound that you say in *hop* and *rob* is called short *o*. Use the symbol *ŏ* to show this sound.

Say these words: **cup   bug.**   Say the vowel sound that you hear in each word. The sound that you say in *cup* and *bug* is called short *u*. Use the symbol *ŭ* to show this sound.

Sometimes a combination of vowels gives you a short vowel sound. For instance, say *head* and *bet*. Both words have the "short E" sound (ě).

Don't just look at a word to determine if it has a short vowel sound. Say it and hear if it sounds like the:

> ă in *man*   (c<u>a</u>p, tr<u>a</u>ck)
> ě in *pet*   (r<u>ea</u>dy, s<u>ay</u>s)
> ĭ in *hit*   (b<u>ui</u>ld, w<u>o</u>men)
> ŏ in *rob*   (w<u>a</u>tch, c<u>a</u>lm)
> ŭ in *cup*   (l<u>o</u>ve, t<u>ou</u>gh)

Now, say each word above, one line at a time. Then say the sounds made by the underlined letters on each line. You will hear how the vowel sounds on each line are the same.

PRACTICE

1. Circle the word in each pair that has the short vowel sound. The first one has been done for you.

    a. ă   (ran)   raid   f. ă   add   ate
    b. ě   bead   rest   g. ě   eight   else
    c. ĭ   still   sight   h. ĭ   island   interest
    d. ŏ   old   job   i. ŏ   opposite   odor
    e. ŭ   upper cute   j. ŭ   use   umbrella

5

2. Circle the two words that have the same short vowel sound. The vowel sounds you are comparing are underlined. The first one has been done for you.

a. (m<u>a</u>t) (h<u>a</u>nd) m<u>a</u>te   **f.** b<u>e</u>d   r<u>e</u>st   r<u>ea</u>l

b. c<u>u</u>t   c<u>o</u>st   h<u>u</u>nk   **g.** l<u>o</u>bby   r<u>o</u>be   r<u>o</u>b

c. <u>i</u>ce   <u>i</u>ll   <u>i</u>nterest   **h.** <u>u</u>ntil   r<u>u</u>st   r<u>u</u>de

d. r<u>oa</u>d   b<u>o</u>ttle   <u>o</u>live   **i.** <u>a</u>ble   <u>a</u>sk   <u>a</u>nt

e. <u>u</u>pper   <u>u</u>se   <u>u</u>s   **j.** s<u>i</u>ck   <u>i</u>tem   s<u>i</u>nk

VC AND VCC PATTERNS

Very often, we will refer to the patterns made by vowels and consonants and the sounds made by those patterns.

Book A of this series introduced the following patterns for short vowel sounds. Remember that V stands for vowels and C stands for consonants.

$$VC = h\underline{at}, m\underline{en}, l\underline{ip}, p\underline{ot}, r\underline{ub}$$

$$VCC = b\underline{ack}, b\underline{est}, l\underline{ick}, r\underline{ock}, b\underline{unch}$$

> IN THE VC PATTERN, A VOWEL AND CONSONANT *END* THE WORD. IN THE VCC PATTERN, A VOWEL AND TWO OR MORE CONSONANTS *END* THE WORD. THESE ARE WORDS WITH SHORT VOWEL SOUNDS.

MORE PRACTICE

Choose the short vowel words in each pattern. Then, indicate whether the short vowel sound word follows the VC or the VCC pattern. The first one has been done for you.

1. ice   (lick)   *VC or* (VCC)
2. hand   hate   *VC or VCC*
3. rob   robe   *VC or VCC*
4. less   lease   *VC or VCC*
5. ape   rat   *VC or VCC*
6. us   cube   *VC or VCC*
7. ill   side   *VC or VCC*
8. king   kite   *VC or VCC*
9. cap   case   *VC or VCC*
10. cope   cost   *VC or VCC*

Short Vowels and Suffixes

You may have to change the form of a short vowel word when you add an ending to it. Some of the most common endings, called **suffixes,** are *-s, -ed,* and *-ing*.

ADDING *S* OR *ES*

For most words, you simply add *s* to the end: *run* ⟶ *runs, stop* ⟶ *stops, exit* ⟶ *exits*. However, look at the words below.

$$\text{wat}\underline{ch} \longrightarrow \text{watch}\underline{es}$$
$$\text{clas}\underline{s} \longrightarrow \text{class}\underline{es}$$
$$\text{da}\underline{sh} \longrightarrow \text{dash}\underline{es}$$
$$\text{bo}\underline{x} \longrightarrow \text{box}\underline{es}$$
$$\text{bu}\underline{zz} \longrightarrow \text{buzz}\underline{es}$$

INSIGHT

Look at the words in the left hand column. What are the underlined letters at the end of each word?

_____ _____ _____ _____ _____

In the right hand column, what ending follows those letters?_____

> ### ADD *ES* TO WORDS ENDING IN *CH, S, SH, X,* AND *Z*.

Notice that when you add *es* to a word, you hear the "IZ sound" at the end of the word. Say the *es* words above and listen for the sound.

PRACTICE

Add *s* or *es* to the following words. The first one has been done for you.

1. box **boxes**
2. risk _____
3. hiss _____
4. path _____
5. rush _____
6. boss _____

7. raft _____
8. fizz _____
9. flash _____
10. watch _____
11. dress _____
12. rest _____

ADDING -ED AND -ING

fan ⟶ fanned ⟶ fanning
list ⟶ listed ⟶ listing

INSIGHT

The words above are short vowel words. The first word, *fan*, is a (*circle one*)   VC   VCC   word.

Do you double the last consonant before you add *-ed* or *-ing*? _____

The second word, *list*, is a (*circle one*)   VC   VCC   word.

Do you double the last consonant before you add *-ed* or *-ing*? _____

> ### FOR VC WORDS *ONLY*, DOUBLE THE FINAL CONSONANT BEFORE ADDING *-ED* OR *-ING*.

MORE PRACTICE

Add *-ed* or *-ing* to the short vowel words below. Double the final consonant if the word ends in VC. The first two have been done for you.

Word	-ed	-ing
1. hop	hopped	hopping
2. pass	passed	passing
3. ask		
4. risk		
5. skip		
6. press		
7. wrap		
8. trust		
9. check		
10. burn		
11. jump		
12. rest		
13. bat		
14. chip		
15. rap		

Alphabetizing

"I can't spell this word."
"Look it up in the dictionary!"
"But if I can't spell it, how can I look it up?"

Does this dialogue sound familiar? If so, don't give up. You **can** find words in the dictionary, even when you aren't sure of their spelling. In this book, you will go step by step through exercises to build your dictionary skills. Let's start with the basics.

You already know the alphabet. Knowing it is the key to using a dictionary because words in a dictionary are listed in alphabetical order. Review the alphabet in your mind before you do the exercise.

PRACTICE

1. **a.** When we put words into alphabetical order, we begin by noticing the first letter of each word. Circle the first letter of each word. The first one has been done for you.

   ⓑeast   weird   also   hate   steal   dictionary

   b. Now take the letters that you circled and find them in the alphabet below. When you find them, put a circle around them.

   a ⓑ c d e f g h i j k l m n o p q r s t
   u v w x y z

   c. You should have circled *a, b, d, h, s,* and *w.* These letters are in alphabetical order. Now write the complete **words** in alphabetical order below. Begin with *also,* since it begins with the letter *a.*

   _____

   _____

   _____

   _____

   _____

   _____

   d. You have just put the words into alphabetical order! Now do the same with the next list. Write them in alphabetical order in your notebook.

   speed   bread   crate   finger   letter   usually

2. a. All of the words below start with the same letter. How do you alphabetize them? No problem—just look at the **second** letter. Circle the second letter of each word. The first one has been done for you.

s(o)cial   see   speak   supper   steak

b. Write the words in alphabetical order, looking at the second letter. Begin with *see*.

_____
_____
_____
_____
_____

c. Now what if you want to add the word *start* to your list? It begins with *st*, just like *steak*. Does it go before or after *steak*? Both words begin with *st*.

    If the first and second letters are the same, you look at the **third** letter: st<u>e</u>ak   st<u>a</u>rt.

Which will go first? _____

Start is the correct answer.

d. Now alphabetize these words in your notebook. Watch out for the second and third letters!

this   that   time   try   to   then

3. Some of the words below start with the same letter, while others start with different letters. Alphabetize this list of words in your notebook, using the first, second, and third letters.

still   letter   look   start   basic   second

_____

Filling Out a Job Application

What is one good reason to spell well? **To get a job!** First impressions are important. If you spell everything correctly on a job application form, the employer will be impressed.

Most job application forms ask you to tell about your work experience: positions you've held, kinds of work you've done, and kinds of businesses you've worked for.

There are so many different words you might need to describe your work experience that it would be impossible to list them all here. To find the spelling of the job words you want to know, answer the questions listed below. If you are working with a class, you and your classmates can do this exercise together, and the instructor can write the words on the blackboard. If you are working on your own, write down the words you want, guessing at the spelling if you are not sure. Then use your dictionary to check the spelling. Use your notebook to write the correct spelling of the words you need.

ANSWER THE QUESTIONS

1. What jobs have you held? (For example: *painter, nurse's aide, laborer.*)

2. What job would you like to have?

3. What kind of businesses have you worked in or for? (For example: *maintenance, hospital, retail sales.*)

4. What kind of business would you like to work in or for?

5. What activities have you performed in your different jobs? (For example: *fix cars, pack boxes, wait on customers.*) Write both present and past forms of the words. (For example: *fix—fixed, pack—packed, wait—waited.*)

6. Why did you leave your jobs? (For example: *health problems, the company closed down.*)

SPECIAL NOTE

a layoff—There was *a layoff* at the factory.

laid off—I was *laid off*. I got *laid off*.

laid off (*past tense*)—The company *laid* me *off*. The factory *laid off* fifty employees.

NOTE TO THE INSTRUCTOR

Be sure that students know both the present and past forms of verbs they might need on job application forms. Students can use the rules they know to form the past of verbs such as *cook* and *ship*. You may need to supply irregular past forms (such as *make—made*) or the past tense spellings of multisyllable words (such as *deliver—delivered*).

Filling out a job application is not just a matter of correct spelling. Use this opportunity to discuss questions that might arise concerning appropriate word choice, explanations, and order of presentation.

PROOFREAD

Check the following job application. Find and correct the errors. The first one has been corrected for you.

FIRM	ADDRESS	DATES WORKED
Betty's Cards & Gifts	321 Main St.	FROM 7/82 TO Present

POSITION HELD: salesperson
~~sellspersin~~

DESCRIBE THE WORK YOU DID: sol gifts, woked as a Kashier, answered the phon

REASON FOR LEAVING: I'm stil workin there, but I wihs to fin a jab with mor opportunities for advancement.

FIRM	ADDRESS	DATES WORKED
Yummy Burgers Restaurant	1517 E. River Rd.	FROM 6/79 TO 5/82

POSITION HELD:

wayter

DESCRIBE THE WORK YOU DID: helpped cook, workked Kash register, waitted on tables, wraped food for carryout

REASON FOR LEAVING:

The restaurant cloze down.

FIRM	ADDRESS	DATES WORKED
Denton's Machine Parts	2700 Industrial Rd.	FROM 2/73 TO 3/79

POSITION HELD:

shiping clerk

DESCRIBE THE WORK YOU DID:
filled oders, chekked shipments, loadded boxs

REASON FOR LEAVING:
I was lay off.

ON YOUR OWN

Complete this partial job application. Don't forget to use the words you chose to write down in your notebook. Be sure to check the spelling of company or street names.

APPLICATION FOR EMPLOYMENT

1. Position you are applying for: _____

    Have you ever done this kind of work? _____

    What is your regular line of work? _____

2. Work Experience: List your last job.

FIRM	ADDRESS	DATES WORKED
		FROM
		TO

    DESCRIBE THE WORK YOU DID:

    REASON FOR LEAVING:

CHAPTER 2

Goals

SOUNDS TO SPELL: Long Vowels
WORD PARTS: Suffixes with Long Vowels
WORDS FOR NOW: Phone Messages
DICTIONARY SKILLS: Guide Words

LONG VOWELS

Mop or Mope (VCe)

You have learned about words with short vowels (ă, ĕ, ĭ, ŏ, ŭ). Now you'll learn about words with long vowels. We show the long vowel sounds like this—ā (as in *fame* or *mail*), ē (as in *keep* or *seam*), ī (as in *bite* or *mice*), ō (as in *vote* or *rose*), and ū (as in *tune* or *cute*). Read each of the words out loud and say the long vowel sound that you hear. Some people remember the long vowel sound by saying that the vowel "says" its name.

SIGHT AND SOUND
Say each word out loud. Note the short vowel sounds in List A and the long vowel sounds in List B.

SAMPLE WORDS
List A   List B

tap ⟶ tape

pet ⟶ Pete

rip ⟶ ripe

not ⟶ note

tub ⟶ tube

INSIGHT

Do the words in List A have short or long vowel sounds? (*Circle one.*)   short   long

Do the words in List B have short or long vowel sounds? (*Circle one.*)   short   long

What vowel/consonant pattern do the words in List A have? _____

NOTE TO THE INSTRUCTOR:
Go through the long vowel sounds with students and have them say words containing each vowel.

The words in List B are similar to the words in List A. We see one vowel and one consonant (VC) in the words on both lists.

But there is one big difference. In List B, what letter is at the end of each word? _____

The silent letter *e* makes the vowel sound long. We will say that the words have the VCe pattern, since they all have one vowel, one consonant, and the letter *e* at the end.

> ## VCe WORDS HAVE LONG VOWELS.

PRACTICE

1. Fill in the missing vowel and the letter *e* for each long vowel word. The first one has been done for you.

   a. A message: n__t__

   b. A large body of water: l__k__

   c. Your watch tells you this: t__m__

   d. A song or melody: t__n__

   e. To elect someone: v__t__

2. Fill in the missing VCe word. The first one has been done for you.

   a. I **hope** you can come to my party.

   b. What is your _____ and address?

   c. Watch out or my dog will _____ you!

   d. At the sound of the _____, the time will be 12:00 noon.

   e. Be polite to your mother. Don't be _____.

   f. He told a dirty _____, but no one laughed.

   g. Shondra took us for a _____ in her new car.

3. Look at each picture and fill in the VCe word. Then think of at least one other VCe word that rhymes. The first one has been done for you.

   a. note   tote, vote _____

   b. _____   _____

   c. _____   _____

   d. _____   _____

PROOFREAD
Find and correct the thirteen mistakes in this letter. The first one has been done for you.

Dear Laura,

     I decided it was ~~tim~~ *time* to send you a little not. I hop you are well. Not much is new with me. Everything is about the sam. The kids and I are fin. Oh yes! David won first priz in an art contest, so we are proud of him.

     I still lik my job, but I hat getting up so early. You know I have to get up at fiv o'clock to get to work on tim. There's only one bus I can tak. Maybe I can sav enough money to get a car.

     Writ soon.

                             Love,
                             Patricia

Suffixes on VCe Words (-S and -ED)

Does Tony **like** me?
Yes. He **likes** you a lot.
He **liked** you before you even met him.

INSIGHT

Look at these words: *like, likes, liked.* The words *like* and *likes* tell about something that is happening now, but the word *liked* tells about something that has already happened—something that happened in the past. Write the correct forms below.

like + s = _____

like + ed = _____

(Note that we really just add the letter *d* to the verb because there is already an *e.*)

What kind of word is *like*? (*Circle one.*)　　VC　　VCC　　VCe

FOR VCe WORDS, JUST ADD -*S* OR -*D* TO MAKE THE
PRESENT OR PAST.

PRACTICE

1. Add -*s* and -*d* to each VCe word below. The first one has been done for you.

   a. like: She **likes**. She **liked**.

   b. bake: He _____. He _____.

   c. vote: She _____. She _____.

   d. file: He _____. He _____.

   e. rule: She _____. She _____.

   f. fade: It _____. It _____.

2. Answer questions about a man you know well. (It could be a friend or a relative.) Add -*d* to each verb.

   EXAMPLE: As a child what did he **like** to do after school?
   He liked to play ball.

   a. As a child, what kind of food did he **like**?

   b. As a child, what did he **hate**?

   c. When he was in high school, whom did he **date**?

   d. Last year, what did he **hope** to do?

   e. Whom did he **vote** for in the last election?

Suffixes on VCe Words (-ING)

Take your time.   **Drive** carefully.
I am **taking** my time.   I am **driving** carefully.

INSIGHT

What kind of words are *take* and *drive*? (*Circle one.*)   VC   VCC   VCe

To add *-ing* to a VCe word like *take* or *drive,* we take away the letter ____ and write ____.

> TO ADD *-ING* TO A VCe WORD, WE TAKE AWAY THE *E*
> AND ADD *-ING*.

PRACTICE

1. Add *-ing* to these words. The first one has been done for you.

   a. take **taking**   f. make _____

   b. vote _____   g. slide _____

   c. write _____   h. joke _____

   d. trade _____   i. shake _____

   e. hope _____   j. tile _____

2. Fill in the missing *-ing* word. Sometimes the first letter has been given to you as a hint. The first one has been done for you.

   a. Right now, I'm **writing** the answers.

   b. The mugger was _____ in the bushes.

   c. She's _____ a cake.

   d. He's _____ into a big, juicy apple.

   e. The sun is **sh**_____.

   f. She's **sm**_____ a cigarette.

   g. He's _____ notes.

   h. She's **w**_____ the tears from her eyes.

Sweet Dreams (VV)

SIGHT AND SOUND

Say each word out loud and listen to the long vowel sound in each.

SAMPLE WORDS

wait tie say

meet boat

INSIGHT

Do these words have short or long vowel sounds? _____

How many vowels does each word have? _____

(The *y* is a vowel here. The letter *y* is a vowel when it comes after another vowel.)

Circle each vowel pair.

We will call these *VV words* since they have two vowels together. There are many different VV combinations, which you'll learn about soon.

> MOST VV WORDS HAVE LONG VOWEL SOUNDS. (SILENT *E* IS NOT NEEDED.)

PRACTICE

In this newspaper report, circle every VV pair you can find. After you have finished, go back and say all of the VV words that you found. (Don't circle the word *said*. It is an exception word. It has two vowels together but has a *short* vowel sound.) The first two have been done for you.

Train Rescue

Three girls, all eleven years old, were discovered locked in a train car after a 300-mile trip. The railroad man who saved them said that faint moans coming from the train car led him to the children.

The girls had climbed into the train car, which was filled with a shipment of beer, and had hidden between the packing crates. "It was OK at first," one girl told reporters. "But then we started to feel hungry and afraid. We were sure we were going to die."

The girls wanted to get off the train but had to stay on for 300 miles. There was nothing else to eat, so they had to have beer to keep alive. "I never want to see another can of beer as long as I live," said another girl.

More Suffixes with Long Vowels

My grandmother is **staying** with us now.

She's going to **stay** with us for three weeks.

She **stays** here every year.

She **stayed** here for two months last year.

stay
stays
stayed
staying

Do you **dream** every night?

No. But my husband **dreams** every night.

Last night he **dreamed** he was a turtle.

dream
dreams
dreamed
dreaming

INSIGHT

What kind of words are *stay* and *dream*? (*Circle one.*)   VC   VCC   VCe   VV

Do we change VV words before adding *-s, -ed,* or *-ing*? (*Circle one.*)   yes   no

> ADD *-S, -ED,* OR *-ING* TO VV WORDS WITHOUT MAKING ANY OTHER CHANGES.

There is one important exception. Add *-es* to any word ending in *-sh* or *-ch.* For example: teach ⟶ teaches

PRACTICE

Circle the two vowels in each VV word. Then add *-s, -ed,* and *-ing* to each. (Watch out for the exception words that take -es instead of *-s.*) The first one has been done for you.

		-s	-ed	-ing
1.	st(ay)	stays	stayed	staying
2.	dream			
3.	rain			
4.	float			
5.	pray			
6.	shield			
7.	cheat			
8.	load			
9.	beep			
10.	reach			
11.	mail			

Suffixes: Double Consonants

TO DOUBLE OR NOT TO DOUBLE?

taping   tapping

1. Are these two words the same? (*Circle one.*)   yes   no

2. Put each word into the correct sentence below.

    Mike is _____ his foot on the floor.

    Sara is _____ the package shut.

    (Check your answers: Mike is tapping . . . . Sara is taping . . . .)

3. Which of the two words comes from *tape*? _____

    Which comes from *tap*? _____

4. Now remember the rule that tells you when to double the consonant: Before *-ing* or *-ed*, we double the final consonant of a (*circle one*)   VC   VCC   VCe   VV   word only.

> REMEMBER: BEFORE *-ED* or *-ING*, DOUBLE THE
> CONSONANT OF A VC WORD **ONLY.**
> (ONE VOWEL, ONE CONSONANT ⟶ DOUBLE.)

Look at how this rule works.

For VC words, we double the final consonant.	For VCC and VV words, we add *-ed* or *-ing* without making any other changes.		For VCe words, we just add *-d* or drop the *-e* and add *-ing*.
VC			**VCe**
tap	**VCC**	**VV**	tape
tapped	help	dream	taped
tapping	helped	dreamed	taping
	helping	dreaming	

PRACTICE

1. Add *-ed* and *-ing* to each word below. (Double the consonant of a VC word only.) To help you remember the correct spelling, write *VC*, *VCC*, *VV*, or *VCe* above each word. The first one has been done for you.

    a. *vc* tap *tapped, tapping*

    b. tape _____

    c. dream _____

    d. walk _____

    e. leak _____

    f. grip _____

g. blame _____   **k.** trick _____

h. want _____   **l.** cope _____

i. need _____   **m.** choke _____

j. rub _____   **n.** slam _____

2. Fill in the missing *-ing* words. The first two have been done for you.

a. John is **writing** (*write*) a letter to his grandmother.

b. Lucille is **stopping** (*stop*) her car at the red light.

c. Michael is _____ (*read*) an interesting story to us.

d. Carrie is _____ (*run*) faster than anyone else in the race.

e. Martin is _____ (*make*) spaghetti for dinner.

f. Sheila enjoys _____ (*drive*) her mother's car.

g. Freddy is _____ (*deal*) the cards.

h. The children are _____ (*play*) in the street.

i. Sandra leaves for work early. When she leaves, her husband is just _____ (*wake*) up.

j. Sandra is tired of _____ (*get*) up so early.

PROOFREAD

Find and correct the fifteen errors in this paragraph. The first one has been done for you.

It's Sunday morning. As I'm ~~wakking~~ waking up, I hear the children talkking and geting out of bed. I know I should get up too, but I love sleeping late. "Five more minutes," I tell myself. Now the children are runing to the kitchen and makeing breakfast. I can hear them takeing out the dishes and droping some on the floor, but still I don't get up. Now they're pourring cereal and milk into their bowls. Soon I hear them eatting.

"One more minute," I say to myself. Now I can hear them washing the dishes and puting them away. "What good kids!" I think. But what's that sound? Drip, drip, drip. They've left the faucet on, and water is driping into the sink. Drip, drip, drip. It's driveing me crazy! I can't stand it anymore. I jump out of bed and run to turn off the water. The children are siting there and smileing at me. "Good morning!" they say.

Phone Messages

Have you ever had to take a phone message at home or at work? When you write a message, you want to spell the words correctly. If you spell everything right, the person who gets the message will be able to read it easily. Also, he or she will have a good impression of you. (This is especially important if the person is your boss!) Here are some telephone words and phrases to learn. Copy the difficult ones in your notebook.

called	this morning
returned your call	this afternoon
wants you to call him/her	this evening
call back	before (10:00 A.M.)
please call	after (10:00 A.M.)
today	between (10:00 A.M. and 2:00 P.M.)
tonight	as soon as possible
tomorrow	urgent
	number
	ext. (extension)

PRACTICE

Complete these messages using the words from the list. Then write your own message. The first one has been done for you.

Michael,

Call Dr.
___1___

Harris. Urgent.

555-6317.

Mrs. Lambert,

Sam Levin _____
___2___

your call.

Tina,

Gregory _____ .
___3___

He _____ you to
___4___

call him back

_____ 5:00 and
___5___

8:00.

Mr. Wilkes,

Harold Endo

_____ you to
___6___

_____ him as
___7___

soon as _____ .
___8___

555-3200, _____
___9___

290.

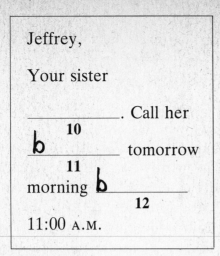

Jeffrey,

Your sister

_____. Call her

b
10
_____ tomorrow
11
morning b
_____
12

11:00 A.M.

PROOFREAD
Now read over these messages and correct the sixteen errors. The first one has been done for you.

Mom,
~~You're~~ **Your** boss call at 10:00 this mornin. Call him bak. 555-4234.

Frankie

Elizabeth,
Coll Gerald tonit befor 8:30. Irgent.

Mrs. Johnson,
Mr. Ryan return you call. Pleas call him betwen 2:00 and 4:00 this afternoon.

R. Hobbes

Mr. Wolek,
Call Darlene Freeman as son as posible. Ugent. 555-1221, etx. 513.

P. Jarvis

PHONE MESSAGE HINTS
Now that you know these special words, it will be easier for you to take phone messages. But there is still one thing that is hard for everyone to spell: names! Of course, some names are easy: Tom Smith, Lisa Brown, and so on. Sometimes there is more than one way to spell a name: Kathryn or Catherine? Marks or Marx? Sometimes the name is difficult because it is long or unusual; for example, Velazquez, Riddiford, Wyszomirski, McKeown, or DiGrazia. Be sure to ask the caller to spell his or her name. Then repeat the spelling to make sure you have written it correctly. Check the telephone number in the same way.

ON YOUR OWN
Now have your instructor or a classmate pretend to call you with a message. Take the message in your notebook.

Guide Words

Did you get frustrated the last time you tried to find a word in the dictionary? Did it seem to take forever to find the page that a word was on?

Pick up your dictionary and open it to any page. Look at the two words at the top of the page. These two words are called **guide words.**

gazette	general
gazette *n* newspaper or official journal	**Gemini** *n* the third zodiac sign
gear *n* equipment or paraphernalia	**gender** *n* sex, as in masculine, feminine, or neuter
geezer *n* an odd or eccentric old man	**gene** *n* a functional hereditary unit made up of DNA or RNA
gelatin *n* a transparent protein obtained from animal tissues by boiling	**general** *adj* of, pertaining to, or affecting the whole
gem *n* precious stone that has been cut and polished for ornamentation	

Notice that the first top word, *gazette,* is the same as the first dictionary entry on the page. Look at the top word on the right side of the page. Where else do you find it? Is it the same as the last entry on the page?

Since the dictionary is in alphabetical order, the guide words will help you to find the page on which you will locate a particular entry.

Let's try one example. Look at the sample dictionary page below. Circle the words below that would appear on this page.

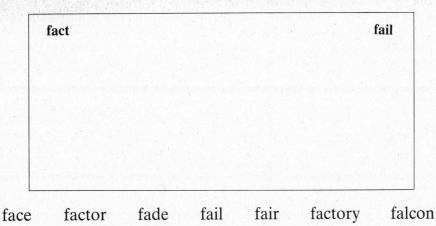

fact   fail

face   factor   fade   fail   fair   factory   falcon

You should have circled *factor, fade, fail* and *factory.*

Let's check two of the words. Fac*e* comes before fac*t* (*e* comes before *t*), so it would not be found on this page.

However, fa*d*e comes after fa*ct* (*d* is after *c*) but before fa*i*l (*d* is before *i*), so it is on the page.

See how important alphabetizing is in dictionary skills!

PRACTICE

1. Look up the following words in your dictionary. For each word, write the guide words for the page where it appears. The first one has been done for you as an example, but the words may be different in your dictionary.

Guide Words

a. **brand**   brave   **bread**

b. _____   people   _____

c. _____   order   _____

d. _____   claim   _____

e. _____   pocket   _____

f. _____   index   _____

g. _____   money   _____

h. _____   mail   _____

2. Circle the guide words that would indicate where a dictionary entry could be found. The first one has been done for you.

a. return   (rest/ribbon)   repeat/reply

b. coin   cohort/coif   coil/cola

c. bed   become/bedlam   bedside/beef

d. radio   rabbit/rail   rag/raincoat

e. lock   look/loud   loaf/log

f. hospital   hose/how   honest/horn

g. home   hive/hold   hole/hoop

h. drive   dress/drink   drill/drop

i. plate   plain/plant   plane/please

j. desert   dessert/deter   deliver/deserves

CHAPTER 3

Goals

SOUNDS TO SPELL: Long Vowels Sound by Sound
WORDS FOR NOW: Numbers
Food Words
DICTIONARY SKILLS: Looking up a Spelling
WORD PARTS: Suffixes after *Y*

LONG VOWELS

Cheers! A Toast! (ō)

You have learned two general long vowel patterns: VCe and VV. Now you'll see how these patterns work with each long vowel. We are going to show you that there are many ways to make the long vowel sounds. You will also learn some special spellings. We begin with ō.

SIGHT AND SOUND

Say each word out loud and notice the "long O" sound (ō).

SAMPLE WORDS

List A	List B
hope	boat
vote	load
broke	moan
code	toast

INSIGHT

What long vowel pattern do you see in List A? (*Circle one.*)   VV   VCe

VCe is the most common pattern for ō.

What long vowel pattern do you see in List B? (*Circle one.*)   VV   VCe

Which two letters together make the VV pattern in List B? ___ ___

> THE "LONG O" SOUND (ō) IS USUALLY SPELLED WITH THE VCe PATTERN. SOMETIMES WE USE THE VV PATTERN WITH THE LETTERS *OA*.

27

WORDS TO LEARN

Here is a list of common *oa* words and some other special spellings. Use the Say-Copy-Check exercise to learn them. Write them in your notebook.

Oa Words		Ost Words	Other Spellings	
coach	groan	host	no	goes
roach	soap	post	go	toe
load	boast	most		hoe
loan	toast	almost		
goal	boat			

WORDS THAT SOUND ALIKE

In your notebook, write a sentence for each word below.

sew: to use a needle and thread
so: very; for that reason (I'm *so* tired. I was hungry, *so* I ate.)

road: street
rode: past of *ride*

sole: bottom of your shoe
soul: your spirit

PRACTICE

Fill in the missing ō words. Watch out for exceptions! Sometimes the first letter is given to you as a hint. The first one has been done for you.

1. To wish: **hope**
2. What you wear over your pajamas: _____
3. A small ship: _____
4. Not all, but _____
5. The person who gives a party: the _____
6. In the middle of a donut, there is a **h**_____.
7. Like a long jacket: _____
8. Money you borrow from a bank: _____
9. Where you live: _____
10. She stubbed her _____.
11. After work, she **g**_____ straight home.
12. An ugly insect that lives in people's homes: _____
13. A dog loves to chew on a _____.
14. He dug up the garden with a _____.
15. You eat this with eggs: _____
16. Something you want to reach in life: _____
17. A funny story you tell: _____

SIGHT AND SOUND

Say each word out loud and listen to the "long O" sound (ō).

SAMPLE WORDS

List A	List B
low	old
blow	cold
grow	sold

INSIGHT

In List A, the words make ō with two letters. What are they? ___ ___

Where do the letters *ow* show up in the word? (*Circle one.*)   beginning   middle   end

(The letters *ow* are a VV pattern. *W* is a vowel when it follows another vowel.)

List B has words with a special spelling. What three letters do you see at the end of each word? ___ ___ ___

> TO SPELL THE "LONG O" SOUND (ō) AT THE END OF A WORD, WE USUALLY WRITE *OW*. *OLD* IS A SPECIAL SPELLING.

WORDS TO LEARN

Use the Say-Copy-Check exercise as you write these words in your notebook.

roll	bolt	owe	bowl
toll	colt	own	don't

WORDS THAT SOUND ALIKE

In your notebook, write a sentence for each word.

no: not yes
know: to have it in your head (I *know* the answer.)

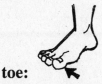

toe:
tow: to pull

MORE PRACTICE

1. Fill in the missing *ow* words. The first one has been done for you.

   a. White stuff that falls from the sky: **snow**

   b. Not high: _____

   c. Not fast: _____

   d. Something people watch: a TV _____

2. Fill in the missing *old* words. The first one has been done for you.
   a. Very brave: **bold**
   b. How _____ are you?
   c. I want to _____ your hand.

3. Fill in the missing word with different spellings of the "long O" sound (ō). The first one has been done for you.
   a. A baby horse: **colt**
   b. How much money do I _____ you?
   c. I'd like a _____ of soup.
   d. Lock and _____ the door.
   e. Do you _____ the answer?
   f. To have or possess: to _____

Now work on all of the ō spellings you have learned.

PROOFREAD

Cross out the word that is spelled wrong. Write the correct spelling on the line. The first one has been done for you.

1. go   no   ~~slo~~   **slow**
2. sope   rope   joke   _____
3. coal   boan   moan   _____
4. loan   foam   boal   _____
5. host   rost   post   _____
6. no   gro   so   _____
7. hoal   goal   groan   _____

MORE PRACTICE

Fill in the missing ō words in the paragraph below. Watch out for special spellings. One letter has been given to you as a hint. The first one has been done for you.

What's your favorite TV **show** ? I like to watch _____
1   2

operas on TV. When I have a bad _____ and can't _____ to
3   4

school, I stay _____ and watch them all day long. I put on my
5

pajamas and my long _____. Then I make some tea and
6

t_____ and sit down to watch. I have been watching one
7

particular show for many years. I have seen some of the actors start

out as children and _____ up into adults. Some of the actors are
8

very _____ now and will probably retire soon. I feel like the
9

actors are my friends. I _____ that the characters aren't real
10

people, but I _____ care.
11

A Close Shave (ā)

SIGHT AND SOUND
Say each word out loud and listen to the "long A" sound (ā).

SAMPLE WORDS

List A	List B	List C
race	fail	day
fade	nail	may
page	gain	pay
shave	train	play

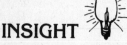

INSIGHT

In List A, what long vowel pattern do you see? _____

In List B, what long vowel pattern do you see? _____

Which two vowels make the VV pattern? _____

Which two consonants follow the letters *ai*? ____ and ____

List C also has words with a VV pattern. Which two letters make the "long A" sound?

_____ _____

Where do the letters *ay* show up in the word? (*Circle one.*)   beginning   middle   end

> TO SPELL THE "LONG A" SOUND (ā), WE USUALLY USE THE VCe PATTERN. BEFORE *L* AND *N*, WE OFTEN WRITE *AI*. AT THE END OF A WORD, WE WRITE *AY*.

WORDS TO LEARN
Use the Say-Copy-Check exercise to write these special *ai* spellings in your notebook.

aid	braid	paid	faint	aim
raid	laid	saint	paint	wait

WORDS THAT SOUND ALIKE
In your notebook, write a sentence for each word below.

made: past of *make*
maid: a woman who cleans

male: a man or boy
mail: letters

plane: airplane
plain: simple

sale: discount

sail:

pane: window glass
pain: hurt

PRACTICE

Fill in *a, ai,* or *ay.* The first one has been done for you.

1. The dog wagged its t___l.
2. Susan m___de a sandwich.
3. He bought a can of spr___ p___nt.
4. You are the m___n reason I st___ in this town.
5. Turn the p___ge.
6. I used to work as a m___d in a hotel.
7. The pl___ne took off at 9:00.
8. Let us pr___.
9. Don't bl___me me!

===========

I just made a loaf of bread. Here, take it!
Wow! It feels like a brick. How much does it **weigh**?
Oh, come on. It's not that bad. Try it! Does it **taste** that **strange**?
No. It's **great**!

Say the dialogue out loud and listen to the words with ā. Then write each bold-type word in the correct list below.

List A	List B	List C	List D
weigh	_____	_____	_____
weight	haste	break	range
eight	paste	steak	change
			stranger

All of the above words have special spellings. Learn them. Copy the words into your notebook using the Say-Copy-Check exercise.

WORDS THAT SOUND ALIKE

In your notebook, write a sentence for each word below.

weight: heaviness
wait: stay in place

weigh: see how heavy something is
way: manner or direction (Do it my *way.* He went that *way.*)

eight: 8
ate: past of *eat*

waste: garbage

waist:

break: **steak:**   **great:** wonderful

brake: **stake:**   **grate:**

MORE PRACTICE

Fill in the correct ā word. These are all special spellings. The first one has been done for you.

1. Go ahead. Don't **wait** for me.

2. Six, seven, _____

3. Eat everything on your plate. It's a sin to _____ food.

4. Be careful not to _____ that vase.

5. I'd love to have a thick, juicy _____ right now.

6. When I saw him, he had a _____ big smile on his face.

7. I lost ten pounds. Now I _____ 150.

8. He put his arm around her _____.

9. Stop the car! Put on the _____!

10. I can't have any dessert. I'm watching my _____.

11. Do you have _____ for a twenty-dollar bill?

Now it is time to remember all the ā spellings that you have learned.

PROOFREAD

Cross out the word that is spelled wrong. Write the correct word on the line. The first one has been done for you.

1. wait   ~~hait~~   maid   **hate**

2. game   late   nale   _____

3. saiv   pain   sail   _____

4. made   rade   fade   _____

5. pay   play   playce   _____

6. waist   taist   wait   _____

7. trane   plane   pane   _____

8. chain   chainge   faint   _____

Looking up a Spelling

Gloria is writing a paragraph. Read what she has written so far.

After all that junk food, I was so sick that I could only ~~mon~~ ~~mone~~ ~~moan~~ cry.

Gloria couldn't remember the correct spelling of a word (*mon, mone,* or *moan*?), so she used a different word (*cry*). Sometimes this is a good idea, but if you do this, you might end up saying something you don't really mean. Instead of changing the word, what could Gloria have done? Of course, she could have asked someone. Better yet, she could have looked up the word in a dictionary. But how could she look up a word if she didn't know how to spell it?

Let's try it ourselves. The first thing to do is to guess the possibilities. Gloria has made three guesses: *mon, mone,* and *moan*. By remembering the spelling rules, we can eliminate one: *mon*. (This VC spelling would give us ŏ, not ō.) We are now left with *mone* and *moan*, which are both possible spellings. To find out which one is right, we simply try to look each one up.

To look for *mone,* we would turn to the page with the correct guide words. (See page 25 to review guide words.) Here is a part of the page.

---

monastery
monastery *n* dwelling place for monks
monaural *adj* monophonic
Monday *n* second day of the week
monetary *adj* of or pertaining to money or to the mechanisms by which it is supplied

---

Do you see *mone* here? No. (If it had been here, it would have been between *Monday* and *monetary*.) So we can be sure that *mone* is not the right spelling. Let's check *moan* now.

---

mixture
mixture *n* the act or process of being mixed
Mo. *n* abbreviation of *Missouri*
m.o. *n* abbreviation of *medical officer*
moan *n* a low, sustained, mournful sound of pain or grief
moat *n* a deep, wide ditch around a fortified place

Do you see it? Yes. It's between *m.o.* and *moat*. If you were Gloria, you could now go back and write the correct word.

Let's try another example:

The police were hot on his trale tral trail.

Of the three guesses, which one would you eliminate? _____
(*Tral* would not have ā because it doesn't have a silent *e*.) Now you would look up both possible spellings, *trale* and *trail*. As it happens, both would fall on the same page. Here is part of that page:

Which spelling is correct? _____

tramp
tragic *adj* dealing with tragedy or any disastrous event
trail *n* trace left by something; scent; track
train *n* a line of connected railroad cars
trait *n* a distinguishing feature or quality
trajectory *n* the path a body makes in space
tram *n* British word for *streetcar*
tramp *n* a begging vagrant; hobo

Now do some more practice. This time use your own dictionary.

PRACTICE
Decide which spellings are possible. Eliminate any spelling that you know is wrong. Then look up the possible spellings and see which one is correct.

EXAMPLE: He bumped his (~~hedd~~, hed, head). **head**

1. I (*hat, hate, hait*) this weather! _____
2. He (*cought, cogth, caught*) the ball. _____
3. This bread is old and (*stail, stal, stale*). _____
4. You must (*sook, soak, soke*) the sweater in the water. _____
5. They (*dread, dredd, dred*) going to the dentist. _____
6. Muggers sometimes (*lork, lirk, lurk*) in dark alleys. _____
7. My (*goal, gole, gol*) is to get my GED. _____
8. The army conducted a (*rad, raid, rade*) on the village. _____
9. Don't (*slirp, slorp, slurp*) your soup. _____

A Fight! A Fight! (ī)

Try some of this **ice** cream.

SIGHT AND SOUND
Say the sentence above out loud and notice the "long I" sound (ī). Then write each bold-type word in the correct list.

SAMPLE WORDS

List A	List B
nice	by
bite	shy
strike	why

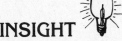

INSIGHT
What spelling pattern do you see in List A? _____

Most ī words have the VCe pattern.

In List B, ī is the last sound in the word. What letter is used to show ī? _____

> MOST "LONG I" (ī) WORDS HAVE THE VCe PATTERN.
> WORDS THAT END IN THE "LONG I" SOUND ARE
> USUALLY SPELLED WITH *Y*.

WORDS TO LEARN
Use the Say-Copy-Check exercise to write these words in your notebook. A few ī words end in *ie*.

die   lie   pie   tie

Here are some other special spellings:

style   guide

WORDS THAT SOUND ALIKE
In your notebook, write a sentence using each word below.

by: I came *by* train.
buy: to pay for something

die: to pass away
dye: to color

I: me
eye: what you see with

PRACTICE
Fill in the missing ī words. Use the VCe pattern, the *y* spelling, or the other special spellings. The first one has been done for you.

1. Do you want beer or <u>wine</u>?

2. She drove _____ our house yesterday.

3. What's the matter? Please don't _____!

4. Not narrow: _____

5. Put some oil in the pan. Then _____ the chicken in the oil.

6. Husband and _____

7. _____ your shoelaces or you'll trip.

8. He went to the store to _____ milk and eggs.

9. I'd like a piece of apple _____.

10. It's not far away. It's less than a _____.

It's so **bright** outside, and I can't **find** my sunglasses!

SIGHT AND SOUND
Say the sentence above out loud and notice the "long I" sound (ī). Then put the bold-type words into the correct lists.

SAMPLE WORDS
List A	List B
_____	_____
kind	right
mind	might
blind	fright

INSIGHT
Lists A and B show two special spellings for ī. What are they? _____ and _____

TWO SPECIAL SPELLINGS FOR THE "LONG I" SOUND ARE *IND* AND *IGHT*.

WORDS TO LEARN
Use the Say-Copy-Check exercise to write these special patterns in your notebook.

Ind	Igh	Ight	Special Ig Spellings	Ild
bind	high	fight	height	mild
blind	sigh	bright	sign	wild
grind	thigh	light		child
		night		

WORDS THAT SOUND ALIKE
In your notebook, write a sentence for each of these words.

write: to use a pen   **hi:** hello   **site:** a place
right: not wrong; not left   **high:** not low   **sight:** vision

MORE PRACTICE

Fill in the missing ī words. All have special spellings. Sometimes the first letter has been given to you as a hint. The first one has been done for you.

1. I can't **find** my glasses.
2. What _____ of TV do you have?
3. Turn on the _____.
4. I **m**_____ go, but I'm not sure yet.
5. He can't see; he's _____.
6. Last _____ I had a bad dream.
7. He's just a little **ch**_____.
8. The airplane is flying _____ above the clouds.
9. What's your _____ ? I'm six feet tall.
10. I'm _____, and you're wrong!

Now it's time to remember all of the ī spellings you have learned.

PROOFREAD

Cross out the ī word that is spelled wrong. Then write the correct spelling on the line. The first one has been done for you.

1. sight   ~~lite~~   might   bite   **light**
2. tide   like   sigh   finne   _____
3. childe   wide   wild   kind   _____
4. bright   nite   flight   kite   _____
5. style   guide   bride   blinde   _____
6. fight   sigth   tie   mind   _____
7. brite   sign   shine   wild   _____

WORD PARTS

Suffixes after Y

I'm **paying** back my loan. I'm **trying** to do it fast.

Write each bold-type word in the correct place.

pay _____   try _____

IF A WORD ENDS IN *Y*, WE JUST ADD *-ING* WITHOUT MAKING ANY OTHER CHANGES.

PRACTICE

Rewrite each of these words with *-ing*. The first one has been done for you.

1. stay **staying**
2. play _____
3. cry _____

4. try _____
5. marry _____
6. study _____

Shawn **played** a good game. He always **plays** well.

Write the two bold-type words.   play ⟶ _____ _____

INSIGHT

In the word *play*, what letter comes before *y*? ____

Is *a* a consonant or a vowel? _____

When we add *-s* or *-ed* to the word, do we change the word in any other way? _____

IF A WORD ENDS IN A VOWEL BEFORE *Y* (VOWEL + *Y*), SIMPLY ADD *-S* OR *-ED* TO THE WORD.

MORE PRACTICE

Add *-s* and *-ed* to each word below. The first one has been done for you.

1. play **plays** **played**
2. stay _____ _____
3. pray _____ _____

4. spray _____ _____
5. stray _____ _____
6. obey _____ _____

Marty **cried** at that movie.
That's strange! He never **cries** at movies.

What word do *cried* and *cries* come from? _____
Write the bold-type words here:

INSIGHT

cry _____ _____

In the word *cry*, what letter comes before *y*? ____

Is *r* a consonant or a vowel? _____

Before the *-s* or *-ed* endings, we change the *y* to ____.

Do we write *-s* or *-es*? ____

WHEN *Y* COMES AFTER A CONSONANT (CONSONANT + *Y*), CHANGE *Y* to *I* AND THEN ADD *-ES* OR *-ED*.

MORE PRACTICE

1. Add *-es* to each word below. The first one has been done for you.

   a. cry **cries**   d. apply _____

   b. try _____   e. marry _____

   c. fly _____

2. Add *-ed* to each word below. The first one has been done for you.

   a. cry **cried**   d. dry _____

   b. fry _____   e. study _____

   c. spy _____

Now remember everything you have learned about adding *-ing*, *-s*, and *-ed* to words ending in *y*.

MORE PRACTICE

Add suffixes to each word below. Make other changes only when necessary. The first two have been done for you.

1. play + ed = **played**   7. pay + ing = _____

2. cry + s = **cries**   8. dry + s = _____

3. try + ing = _____   9. fry + ed = _____

4. stay + ed = _____   10. pray + s = _____

5. fly + s = _____   11. study + ing = _____

6. spy + ing = _____   12. marry + ed = _____

Numbers

Have you ever written a check? Do you think you might write a check in the future? Take a look at this one:

```
                                                              101
    JAMES C. MORRISON
      1765 SHERIDAN DRIVE
      YOUR CITY, U.S.A.  12345          Jan. 2  19 86   00-6789
                                                         2345
PAY TO THE
ORDER OF  Dr. J. Slotkin                        $ 27.00
  Twenty-seven and 00/100 ————————————————— DOLLARS

  DELUXE National State Bank
    Your City, U.S.A. 12345
                                        James Morrison
MEMO_____

o|:2345m6789|: 12345678m|
```

A check is an example of different ways to write numbers. We often use figures (*27*). But sometimes we need to write out the word (*twenty-seven*). Use the Say-Copy-Check exercise to copy these numbers into your notebook.

1: one	11: eleven	21: twenty-one	40: forty
2: two	12: twelve	22: twenty-two	50: fifty
3: three	13: thirteen	23: twenty-three	60: sixty
4: four	14: fourteen	24: twenty-four	70: seventy
5: five	15: fifteen	25: twenty-five	80: eighty
6: six	16: sixteen	26: twenty-six	90: ninety
7: seven	17: seventeen	27: twenty-seven	100: one hundred
8: eight	18: eighteen	28: twenty-eight	200: two hundred
9: nine	19: nineteen	29: twenty-nine	300: three hundred
10: ten	20: twenty	30: thirty	400: four hundred

PRACTICE

1. Write the correct number. The first one has been done for you.

a. 7 **seven**

b. 4 _____

c. 13 _____

d. 2 _____

e. 15 _____

f. 19 _____

g. 20 _____

h. 28 _____

i. 35 _____

j. 53 _____

2. Complete each check by writing the correct number on the line. The first one has been done for you.

a.

JAMES C. MORRISON
1765 SHERIDAN DRIVE
YOUR CITY, U.S.A. 12345

102

May 16 19*86*   00-6789 / 2345

PAY TO THE
ORDER OF *Jill N. Lispin* $ *800.00*

Eight hundred and 00/100 _____ DOLLARS

DELUXE National State Bank
Your City, U.S.A. 12345

James Morrison

MEMO_____

1:2345 m 6789 1: 1234 5678 0

b.

JAMES C. MORRISON
1765 SHERIDAN DRIVE
YOUR CITY, U.S.A. 12345

103

_____ 19____   00-6789 / 2345

PAY TO THE
ORDER OF_____ $ *20.34*

_____ *and* 34/100 _____ DOLLARS

DELUXE National State Bank
Your City, U.S.A. 12345

MEMO_____

1:2345 m 6789 1: 1234 5678 ui

c.

JAMES C. MORRISON
1765 SHERIDAN DRIVE
YOUR CITY, U.S.A. 12345

104

_____ 19____   00-6789 / 2345

PAY TO THE
ORDER OF_____ $ *43.98*

_____ *and* 98/100 _____ DOLLARS

DELUXE National State Bank
Your City, U.S.A. 12345

MEMO_____

1:2345 m 6789 1: 1234 5678 ui

d.

JAMES C. MORRISON
1765 SHERIDAN DRIVE
YOUR CITY, U.S.A.   12345

105

_____ 19____   00-6789 / 2345

PAY TO THE
ORDER OF_____ $ *12.27*

_____ *and* $\frac{27}{100}$ _____ DOLLARS

DELUXE National State Bank
Your City, U.S.A. 12345

MEMO_____   _____

⑈⑆2345⑈6789⑆ 12345678⑈

---

e.

JAMES C. MORRISON
1765 SHERIDAN DRIVE
YOUR CITY, U.S.A.   12345

106

_____ 19____   00-6789 / 2345

PAY TO THE
ORDER OF_____ $ *32.00*

_____ *and* $\frac{00}{100}$ _____ DOLLARS

DELUXE National State Bank
Your City, U.S.A. 12345

MEMO_____   _____

⑈⑆2345⑈6789⑆ 12345678⑈

---

f.

JAMES C. MORRISON
1765 SHERIDAN DRIVE
YOUR CITY, U.S.A.   12345

107

_____ 19____   00-6789 / 2345

PAY TO THE
ORDER OF_____ $ *200.00*

_____ *and* $\frac{00}{100}$ _____ DOLLARS

DELUXE National State Bank
Your City, U.S.A. 12345

MEMO_____   _____

⑈⑆2345⑈6789⑆ 12345678⑈

Am I Blue? (ū or o͞o)

Jason is acting crazy.
I know. That **fool** belongs in the **zoo.**

Say the dialogue. Listen to the o͞o sound in *fool* and *zoo*. What two letters spell the o͞o sound?

> THE LETTERS *OO* ARE OFTEN USED TO SPELL THE o͞o SOUND.

WORDS TO LEARN

Here are some common o͞o words. Use the Say-Copy-Check exercise to copy them into your notebook.

Oo	Ool	Oom	Oon	Oot	Other
boo	cool	boom	moon	boot	food
moo	spool	bloom	noon	loot	choose
too	school	groom	soon	root	proof
zoo			spoon	shoot	groove

There are some o͞o words with only one *o* or the *ou* combination. Use the Say-Copy-Check exercise to copy these into your notebook.

do   who   whom   tomb   womb   move   movie   prove   shoe

group   soup   through   you   youth

WORDS THAT SOUND ALIKE

In your notebook, write a sentence for each of these words.

to: opposite of *from* (Go **to** bed.)
too: also
two: 2

Watch out for these words that sound almost alike:

lose: leave something behind (Don't *lose* your keys.)
loose: not tight (These shoes are too *loose*.)

PRACTICE

Fill in the missing o͞o words. Be careful; some have special spellings. The first one has been done for you.

1. There are many animals at the <u>zoo</u>.

2. They bought a lot of _____ at the supermarket.

3. Good morning. How are _____?

4. They're watching TV in the living _____.

5. I _____ my temper too easily.

6. I will _____ to you that I am innocent.

7. The park has a new swimming _____.

8. Blow on the soup to _____ it off.

9. Don't talk to him. He's in a bad _____.

10. He took off his left _____ and rubbed his foot.

11. Stop! Don't _____ that gun!

12. There was a _____ of teenagers standing on the corner.

13. The train went _____ the tunnel.

14. You're tired, and I'm tired, _____.

You have just studied words that have the o͞o sound, like *zoo* and *food.* Now let's look at a slightly different sound. If you say the words *cute* and *few,* you hear the "YOO" sound (ū). There are some words that can be pronounced either way, depending on the part of the country you're from. To find out how to spell them, work through the next exercise.

SIGHT AND SOUND
Say each word out loud and notice the o͞o or ū sound. (The first word in each list has the ū sound; the second word has the o͞o sound. The third can be pronounced either way.)

SAMPLE WORDS

List A	List B	List C
cute	cue	few
rule	glue	crew
tune	due	new

> TO SPELL THE o͞o OR ū SOUND, WE USE THE LETTER
> *U* IN THE VCe PATTERN. WHEN THE o͞o OR ū SOUND
> IS AT THE END OF A WORD, WE USE *OO, UE,* OR *EW.*

WORDS TO LEARN
Use the Say-Copy-Check exercise to copy these words into your notebook.

VCe		Ue	Ew	
dude	fuse	cue	few	crew
nude	cute	due	pew	drew
rude	mute	clue	chew	grew
rule	flute	glue		stew
tune	crude	true		

Some words have special spellings. Copy them into your notebook.

beauty   beautiful   suit   fruit   juice   bruise   view   truth

WORDS THAT SOUND ALIKE

In your notebook, write a sentence for each of these words.

blue: a color
blew: past of *blow*

new: not old
knew: past of *know*

flu: a sickness
flew: past of *fly*

through: He walked *through* the park.
threw: past of *throw*

MORE PRACTICE

1. Fill in the missing VCe words. In one case, the first letter has been given to you as a hint. The first one has been done for you.

   a. He played a _tune_ on the piano.

   b. You'll have to _____ the other door. This one is broken.

   c. Your baby is so _____!

   d. A _____ is a musical instrument.

   e. He blew a _____ when he turned on everything at once.

   f. Remember the golden _____: do unto others as you would have them do unto you.

2. Fill in the missing *ue* or *ew* words. (Check the "Words to Learn" list.) The first one has been done for you.

   a. The fingerprint was an important _clue_.

   b. They had beef _____ for dinner.

   c. You might not believe this, but it's _____. It really happened.

   d. You have only a _____ minutes left.

   e. My mother _____ up in a small town.

   f. When you play pool, you use a stick called a _____.

   g. The American flag is red, white, and _____.

   h. I got 100 percent on the test because I _____ all the answers.

3. Fill in the missing o͞o or ū words with special spellings. The first one has been done for you.

   a. _Beauty_ is only skin deep.

   b. He wore a _____ and tie.

   c. Would you like some orange _____ to drink?

   d. I fell down. Now I have a big purple _____ on my leg.

e. She is the most _____ woman I have ever seen. Everyone looks at her when she walks down the street.

f. From the top of the building, you get a _____ of the whole city.

g. Carrots are my favorite vegetable, and apples are my favorite _____.

Where's the Beef? (ē)

I need to **see** a doctor!

Read the sentence out loud and listen to the "long E" sound (ē).

INSIGHT

What long vowel pattern appears in *need* and *see*? (*Circle one.*)   VCe   VV

Which two vowels together make the "long E" sound? _____

> ### TO WRITE THE "LONG E" SOUND (ē), WE OFTEN USE THE VOWEL LETTERS *EE*.

WORDS TO LEARN

Here is a list of common *ee* words.

Ee	Eed	Eep	Eet	Other
fee	need	keep	feet	beef
tree	bleed	sheep	meet	week
three		sleep	sweet	feel

A few words use only one *e* to make the ē.

he   me   we   she

WORDS THAT SOUND ALIKE

In your notebook, write a sentence for each of these words.

be: He might **be** sick.
bee: It can sting you.

PRACTICE

Fill in the missing *ee* words. The first one has been done for you.

1. I can't **see** without my glasses.
2. Joe got stung by a _____.
3. The _____ limit is 55 mph.
4. The bird was singing in the _____.
5. The baby is hungry. I'd better _____ her.
6. I _____ sick.
7. Do you _____ any help?
8. Seven days make a _____.

You can get a **cheap meal** at Kelly's. Children can **eat** for $2.50 **each.**

Say the sentences above out loud and listen to the "long E" sound (ē).

INSIGHT

What long vowel pattern do you see in the bold-type words? (*Circle one.*)   VCe   VV

What two vowels together make the "long E" sound? _____ _____

> TO WRITE THE "LONG E" SOUND (ē), WE OFTEN USE THE
> VOWEL LETTERS *EA.*

WORDS TO LEARN
Here is a list of common *ea* words.

beach	speak	steal	clean	least	seat
teach	real	mean	tea	rear	heat

MORE PRACTICE
Fill in the missing *ea* words. The first one has been done for you.

1. This isn't expensive. It's **cheap** .
2. Do you want coffee or _____?
3. They went swimming at the _____.
4. She can _____ French.
5. _____ up your room!
6. Can you _____ me how to drive?
7. The opposite of *most* is _____.
8. Please come in and have a _____ on the sofa.
9. It's cold in here. Turn on the _____.
10. Please move to the _____ of the bus.
11. Is that a _____ diamond or a fake?
12. I'm afraid someone will _____ my bike.
13. What does this word _____?

MORE WORDS TO LEARN
A few ē words have special spellings. Write them in your notebook.

key   people   brief   chief   grief   thief   field   pizza

police   ski   weird

WORDS THAT SOUND ALIKE

There are many ē words that sound the same but are spelled differently. Here are some of the most common. In your notebook, write a sentence for each.

beat: to hit
beet: a vegetable

steal: to rob
steel: a metal

heal: to cure or make better

meet: to get together with someone

heel:

meat:

weak: not strong
week: seven days

hear: to listen
here: not there

sea: ocean
see: look

peace: not war
piece: a part or slice

seam: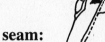

seem: You **seem** tired.

MORE PRACTICE

Circle the correct word for each sentence. The first one has been done for you.

1. Can you (*sea, see*) the blackboard?
2. Last (*weak, week*) I bought a car.
3. I like (*meat, meet*) and potatoes.
4. I can't (*hear, here*) you.
5. The (*heal, heel*) of her shoe came off.
6. You don't (*seam, seem*) very happy to me.
7. He is too (*weak, week*) to get out of bed.
8. Let's (*meat, meet*) at the restaurant at 6:30.
9. It's cruel to (*beat, beet*) your children.
10. Come over (*hear, here*).
11. He can (*heal, heel*) the sick.

PROOFREAD

There are sixteen ē words spelled wrong in the paragraph below. Find them and correct them. The first one has been done for you.

~~feel~~
~~fel~~ When I first came to this town, I didn't know anyone. I used to fel so lonely. I would aet my meels alone and reed the newspaper because I had no one to speek to. Every weak I would go out and sea a movie because I had to do something with my fre time. Of course, I wanted to meat some new peple, but I didn't know how. Then one day on the bus, I started to go to slep. Suddenly I thought someone was trying to stael my umbrella. I opened my eyes and saw a young woman with her hand on my umbrella. "That belongs to mi!" I said. She said, "I'm sorry. I thought it was mine. I'm not a theif, you know. Hear is your umbrella." We began to talk, and that's how I met my first reel friend.

WORD GAMES
Crossword Puzzle

Read each clue and write the ē word in the correct place in the puzzle. In some cases, the first letter is given to you as a hint.

Across

2. Look before you _____.

3. What do you want to _____ when you grow up?

4. Ocean

6. The movie was so sad that it brought _____ to my eyes.

7. To cure or make better

8. You work in that school? What subject do you _____?

9. She can _____ and write well.

11. If you plant an acorn, an oak _____ will grow.

12. Not fake

14. I'm a vegetarian. I don't eat _____.

15. _____ and every one

16. He broke the car window and tried to _____ the radio.

17. Sit in your _____.

Down

1. Take two aspirin and call _____ in the morning.

2. Our roof has a _____. When it rains, water drips in.

3. When I go to the ocean, I like to lie on the _____ in the bright sun.

4. Go down this _____, and then turn right at the light.

5. Not expensive

6. One, two, _____

8. There are nine players on a baseball _____.

9. _____ out and touch someone.

10. What you have while asleep

13. Opposite of most

15. What did you _____ for lunch?

Feel the Chill (ē, ĭ)

Sometimes clear pronunciation can help you spell better.

SIGHT AND SOUND
Say each word out loud. Begin with the first word in List A with the "long E" sound (ē). Then say the word across from it in List B with the "short I" sound (ĭ). Do the same thing until you finish the lists.

SAMPLE WORDS

List A	List B
feel	fill
feeling	filling
peel	pill
meal	mill
teen	tin

PRONUNCIATION NOTE
Sometimes people mix up the spellings of ē and ĭ words, especially when they come before the letter *l*. If you clearly pronounce the ē and ĭ words, your spelling will be correct.

WORDS THAT SOUND ALIKE
There are some ē and ĭ words that sound alike. Write a sentence for each of these words in your notebook.

ē	ĭ
feel: I *feel* good. ——————→	**fill:** *Fill* up the tank.
heel:	**hill:**
peel: *Peel* the potatoes.	**pill:** Take your *pill*.
seal: *Seal* the envelope.	**sill:** window *sill*
we'll: *We'll* go with you.	**will:** I *will* go.
steal: rob	**still:** She *still* plays with dolls.
steel: a metal	
seat: a chair	**sit:** not stand
sleep: what you do at night	**slip:** Don't *slip* on the ice.
feet: the things in your shoes	**fit:** be the right size
sheep:	**ship:**
these: *these* books (more than one)	**this:** *this* book (only one)

leave: go out   **live:** I *live* in Florida.

leap: to jump   **lip:** the outside of your mouth

PRACTICE

Fill in the correct ē or ĭ words. The first two have been done for you.

1. I hope you **feel** better soon.
2. The doctor sent me a **bill**.
3. Watch out with that gun! You might _____ someone by mistake.
4. He slipped on a banana _____.
5. Which is your favorite _____: breakfast, lunch, or dinner?
6. She put the flowers on the window _____.
7. _____ out this application.
8. It's the _____ thing.
9. Johnny is six years old, but he _____ sucks his thumb.
10. These pots and pans are made out of _____.
11. My uncle has twenty _____ on his farm.
12. These shoes don't _____ my _____.
13. That isn't a mountain. It's a _____.
14. The high school students are giving a _____ party.
15. His wife has a headache. That's why he gave her a _____.
16. _____ have to buy ourselves some new hats.
17. The sailors are waving good-bye from the _____.
18. How much are _____ strawberries going to cost?
19. That old man is going to _____ on the ice.
20. Please save me a _____ next to you.

ON YOUR OWN

In your notebook, write a sentence with each of these words.

1. fill
2. feel
3. real
4. still
5. live
6. leave
7. sleep
8. sit

Food Words

How often do you think about food? At least three times a day! Sometimes you have to write about food, too. If you make shopping lists, write down recipes, or sell food, you'll need to know how to spell the words correctly.

But how many different kinds of food are there? Hundreds! How can you find out how to spell the words you need? A cookbook is your best source. Take a cookbook from your home or borrow one from a library. Then turn to the back and find the index. (The index is the list at the back of a book that tells you how to find information on different topics. The index is in alphabetical order, just like a dictionary.) Here you will find many of the food words you need to know. Copy the ones you want to learn into your notebook.

Now try these exercises. Use your cookbook (and your dictionary) to help you.

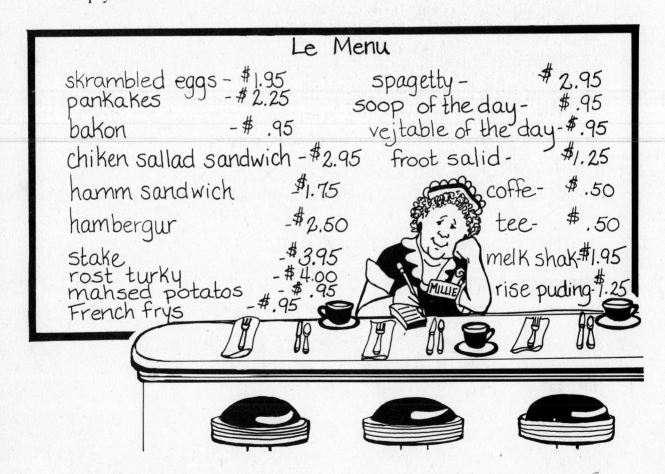

Le Menu

skrambled eggs - $1.95
pankakes - $2.25
bakon - $ .95
chiken sallad sandwich - $2.95
hamm sandwich $1.75
hambergur - $2.50
stake - $3.95
rost turky - $4.00
mahsed potatos - $ .95
French frys - $ .95

spagetty - $2.95
soop of the day - $ .95
vejtable of the day - $ .95
froot salid - $1.25
coffe - $ .50
tee - $ .50
melk shak - $1.95
rise puding - $1.25

PROOFREAD

Millie runs a restaurant that serves delicious food. The only problem is that people have trouble reading her menu. Find and correct all of Millie's spelling errors.

_____

_____

_____

_____

_____

_____

_____

_____

_____

_____

_____

_____

_____

_____

_____

_____

ON YOUR OWN

1. In your notebook, make a list of foods you want to buy at the supermarket.

2. Imagine that a group of your friends is coming over to your house for dinner. What will you make? Plan your dinner party. In your notebook, make a list of everything you'll serve.

3. How is your diet? In your notebook, write down what you should eat more of and what you shouldn't eat so much of.

    EXAMPLE: I should eat more oranges.
    I shouldn't eat so much bacon.
    I shouldn't eat so many cookies.

57

CHAPTER 4

Goals

SOUNDS TO SPELL: Consonant Combos
DICTIONARY SKILLS: Finding the Right Spelling
WORD PARTS: Plurals
WORDS FOR NOW: Days and Months
WORDS TO USE: Possessive Nouns

CONSONANT COMBOS

Snatch a Smooch (CH)

We've looked carefully at vowel spellings. Now it's time to focus on the combinations of consonants. We will focus on pairs of consonants that make only one sound. While you practice consonant spellings, keep in mind all the **vowel** spellings you've learned: VC, VCC, VCe, and VV. You'll use these patterns in combination with the consonant spellings.

If you can **catch** me, I'll give you a **smooch**!

SIGHT AND SOUND
Say the sentence above out loud. Then write each bold-type word in the correct list.

SAMPLE WORDS

List A	List B
peach	pitch
coach	scratch

INSIGHT

In List A, how many vowels do you see in each word? _____

Which two letters make the "CH" sound? ____ ____

Circle the two vowels (VV) and underline the *ch* in each word.

In List B, how many vowels do you see in each word? _____

Which three letters make the "CH" sound? ____ ____ ____

Circle the single vowel and underline the *tch* in each word.

> AFTER TWO VOWELS TOGETHER, WRITE *CH* TO MAKE THE "CH" SOUND. AFTER A SINGLE VOWEL, WRITE *TCH*.

SPECIAL NOTE

Even though most words follow the above pattern, there are some exceptions, such as *much, rich, such,* and *which.*

PRACTICE

Fill in *ch* or *tch*. The first one has been done for you.

1. pea**ch**
2. la_____
3. cou_____
4. tea_____
5. sti_____
6. rea_____
7. bea_____
8. clu_____
9. slou_____

PROOFREAD

Cross out the word that is spelled wrong. Write the correct spelling on the line. The first one has been done for you.

1. ~~reatch~~   patch   match   **reach**
2. latch   pitch   coutch   _____
3. touch   cach   peach   _____
4. teatch   pouch   scratch   _____
5. stretch   hatch   bleatch   _____
6. rich   much   cruch   _____
7. pich   which   such   _____

Pass the Butter Please (SS, SE)

SIGHT AND SOUND
Say each word out loud. Notice the "S" sound in List A. Notice the "S" or "Z" sound in List B.

SAMPLE WORDS

List A	List B
pass	please
mess	cheese
loss	loose

INSIGHT
What pattern do you see in each word in List A? (*Circle one.*) VC VCC VCe VV

How many vowels are in each word? _____

Which letters make the "S" sound? ____ ____

Circle the vowel and underline the *ss*.

What pattern do you see in each word in List B? (*Circle one.*) VC VCC VCe VV

How many vowels do you see together before the *s*? _____

Which letter makes the "S" or "Z" sound? _____

Which letter comes after the *s*? _____

Circle the two vowels together and underline the *se*.

> IN WORDS WITH A SINGLE SHORT VOWEL, WRITE *SS* AND SAY THE "S" SOUND. IN VV WORDS, WRITE *SE* AND SAY THE "S" SOUND OR THE "Z" SOUND.

PRACTICE
Fill in the *ss* or *se*. The first one has been done for you.

1. plea**se**
2. pa____
3. le____
4. moo____
5. brui____
6. cro____
7. lea____
8. dre____

PROOFREAD

Cross out the word that is spelled wrong. Write the correct spelling on the line. The first one has been done for you.

1. press   ~~pleasse~~   tease   **please**

2. goose   grass   greass   _____

3. noose   chooss   cross   _____

4. lease   toss   blesse   _____

5. passe   kiss   noise   _____

6. cheez   chess   mess   _____

7. boss   masse   cruise   _____

Finding the Right Spelling

Have you been using your dictionary more than before? If so, that's great! If not, keep in mind that a dictionary can help you to spell words on your own. You can find the right spelling of words **yourself** and you won't have to ask other people for help all the time.

Let's review some of the dictionary skills.

REVIEW PRACTICE

1. In the dictionary, words are listed in *alphabetical order.* In your notebook, put these words into alphabetical order.

   a. small   zone   youth   young   think

   b. fact   face   fall   fake   famous

   c. warm   want   war   wait   wad

2. Remember that *guide words* at the top of each dictionary page can help you find the word you want. For each word on the left, circle the correct guide words. The first one has been done for you.

   a. city   circuit/citizen   (citric/clamp)

   b. kind   kill/king   kingdom/kitten

   c. light   lift/likelihood   likely/linchpin

   d. public   prow/psychotic   pub/puff

   e. year   yard/yearn   yeast/yokel

   f. thought   they/thistle   thong/threw

   g. often   ocean/of   off/oil

MORE PRACTICE

Let's work with a common problem. How do you look up words that you don't already know how to spell? What if there is more than one possible way to spell a sound? You can look up the different possibilities to see which is correct.

1. A student wrote the following sentence but did not know how to spell one of the words. She did, however, write down some of the different ways that the word could be spelled.

   The car drove down the rod? road? rode?

   Rod won't work. It has the VC pattern, so it has a short vowel. The word that she wants has a long vowel sound.

The next possibility is *road.* If you look up the word *road* in the dictionary, you will find that it means "a way made for traveling." That's our word!

Check the last word just to make sure you got the right one. For *rode,* the dictionary says, "past tense of *ride.*" *Rode* is a word, but it's not the word you want.

2. In the following sentences, look at the three spelling guesses. If one is impossible, eliminate it right away. Then look up the two possibilities that are left. Use your own dictionary. Write the correct spelling on the line. The first one has been done for you.

   a. That was the (*first, furst, fist*) thing I did. first

   b. Don't be so (*mene, mean, menn*)! _____

   c. There are five players on a basketball (*team, tem, teme*). _____

   d. He wants to (*shaive, shav, shave*) his head. _____

   e. The car skidded down the (*slop, slope, sloap*). _____

   f. The cat started to (*prol, prowl, proull*). _____

   g. There was a (*groop, group, grop*) of teenagers. _____

   h. He bought a (*dowel, dowl, doul*) rod at the lumberyard. _____

   i. Put on your coat or you'll (*freaz, frez, freeze*). _____

   j. She got a (*stain, stane, stann*) on her skirt. _____

   k. We still (*greeve, grieve, griv*) for our cousin who passed away last year. _____

Plurals

We went to the country for our summer vacation
and saw lots of beautiful **hills, fields,** and
beaches. The only problem was the **flies!**

Read the sentences above out loud. Notice the bold-type plural forms.
(Remember that *singular* means one and *plural* means more than one.)
Now write each plural form next to the singular word below.

hill **hills**   beach _____

field _____   fly _____

Do you remember the rules for adding the plural -*s* to words? Remember
the rules:

We just add (*circle one*)   -s   -es   to most words.

We add (*circle one*)   -s   -es   to words ending in *s, z, ch, sh,* and
x.

If the word ends in *y* after a (*circle one*)   consonant   vowel
change the *y* to _____ and add -*es.*

SPECIAL NOTES

1. Remember that, if *y* comes after a **vowel,** we just add -*s* without
    changing anything else. For example: boy _____; day _____

2. There is one special spelling to learn: *quiz* ⟶ *quizzes.* This is an
    exception to the rules.

PRACTICE
Fill in the plural form of these words. The first three have been done for
you.

1. field **fields**
2. beach **beaches**
3. fly **flies**
4. joint _____
5. lake _____
6. church _____
7. spy _____
8. bus _____
9. belt _____
10. box _____
11. dress _____
12. tray _____
13. bag _____
14. toy _____
15. lady _____
16. quiz _____

Did you know Bentley's **wife?**
Which one? He had three **wives,** you know, and they all left him.

SIGHT AND SOUND
Read the dialogue above out loud. Then write the bold-type words in the correct places in the lists.

SAMPLE WORDS
Singular	Plural
___	___
life	lives
shelf	shelves

INSIGHT

How many times does *f* show up in each singular word? ___

What letter is used instead of *f* in each plural word? ___

After *v,* do we write *-s* or *-es*? ___

> MANY WORDS ENDING IN *F* OR *FE* CHANGE TO *VES* IN THE PLURAL.

MORE PRACTICE
Fill in the plural form of each word. The first one has been done for you.

1. wife **wives**
2. knife ___
3. shelf ___
4. leaf ___
5. half ___

6. scarf ___
7. life ___
8. calf ___
9. loaf ___
10. thief ___

SPECIAL NOTES
1. Learn the *ves* plural words in the exercise above. They are the most common. For some other *f* or *fe* words, just add *-s*. For example:

   chief **chiefs**   belief ___

2. If the word ends in *ff,* just add *-s*. For example:

   cuff **cuffs**   puff ___

3. Some words end in *o*. Here are some examples:

   radio   stereo   zoo   piano   banjo

   To make them plural, we just add *-s:*

   radio **radios**   piano ___

   stereo ___   zoo ___

   photo ___   rodeo ___

65

For a few common words ending in *o*, add *-es*. Copy them into your notebook.

$$hero \longrightarrow heroes$$
$$potato \longrightarrow potatoes$$
$$tomato \longrightarrow tomatoes$$

IRREGULAR PLURALS

I have only one **child,** but my sister has four **children.**

INSIGHT

Which bold-type word is singular? _____

Which bold-type word is plural? _____

Do you see *-s* on the end of the plural word? _____

> SOME WORDS HAVE SPECIAL PLURAL FORMS. (THESE ARE CALLED *IRREGULAR PLURALS.*) THEY DO NOT USE *-S.*

Use the Say-Copy-Check exercise to copy all of these words into your notebook. (Copy the singular forms too.)

Singular	Plural
child	children
man	men
woman	women
person	people
foot	feet
tooth	teeth
mouse	mice

MORE PRACTICE

Look at each picture and fill in the correct singular or plural form of the missing word. Use the words in the list above. The first one has been done for you.

1. one <u>child</u>

2. two _____

3. three <u>w</u>

66

4. one _____

5. four _____

6. two _____

7. one _____

8. three _____

9. many _____

10. one _____

OTHER IRREGULAR PLURALS

A few animal names do not change from singular to plural. Use the Say-Copy-Check exercise to copy them into your notebook.

one sheep ⟶ two sheep   one deer ⟶ two deer

one fish ⟶ two fish

Note: Webster's Dictionary also lists *fishes* as an acceptable second spelling.

PROOFREAD

In this paragraph, there are twenty-three words that should be plural. Find them and make them plural. The first one has been done for you.

I'm one of those ~~person~~ people with a terrible habit. No, I'm not like those woman who smoke and drink or like those man who take drugs. What's my habit? I collect thing. If you come to my house, you'll see three or four pile of book stacked by the door. Then, if you look inside my closet, you'll see about ten coat and about twenty old shoe and sandal. My living room is only about ten foot long, but it has two couch and five chair. My coffee table has at least three ashtray for all my guest who smoke and also two lamp so there'll be enough light. Look at one wall, and you'll see thirty or more photo of all my baseball hero, like Pete Rose, Hank Aaron, and Roberto Clemente. Look at another wall and you'll see many postcard of all the city I've visited, like New York, L.A., and Chicago. Walk into my kitchen, and you'll see I collect food. On all the shelf of my refrigerator, you'll find jar of leftover. I don't always eat them, but I can't throw them away until they start to turn green. As you can tell, I live by myself. Sometimes I think I'd like to get married and have a few child, but where would I find the space?

Three Months (TH)

SIGHT AND SOUND

Say each word out loud. Be sure to pronounce the "TH" sound.

SAMPLE WORDS

(th)ink	ma(th)
thank	health
three	bath
throw	month

INSIGHT

Which two letters together make the "TH" sound? _____

Circle the letters *th* in each word.

> TO WRITE THE "TH" SOUND, WE ALWAYS USE THE LETTERS *TH*.

PRONUNCIATION NOTE

The "TH" sound is a special sound, different from the "T" sound, the "S" sound, and the "F" sound. To say the "TH" sound, put your tongue between your teeth. If you can say the "TH" sound clearly, it will be easier for you to spell words that have *th*.

SPECIAL NOTE

Here are some more words to watch out for. Use the Say-Copy-Check exercise to write them in your notebook.

thin: not fat

fin:
tin: a metal

bath:

bat:

thick: not thin
sick: ill
tick: the sound a clock makes

fought: past of *fight*
thought: past of *think*

death: opposite of *life*
deaf: cannot hear

threw: past of *throw*
through: He walked *through* the park.

three: 3

tree: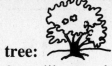

free: liberated; without charge (A slave is not *free*. Here is a *free* sample.)

PRACTICE

Fill in the missing words that start or end with *th*. The first one has been done for you.

1. Please __thaw__ out the frozen chicken so we can cook it for dinner.

2. _____ you very much.

3. He is sick with a sore _____.

4. Is the cake done yet? No, I don't _____ so.

5. _____ the ball to me.

6. I'm hot and _____. I need a drink of water.

7. What are you doing here? I _____ you had gone home.

8. The train went _____ the tunnel.

9. The dust was an inch _____ in some places.

10. Go take a _____—you're too dirty.

11. After her husband's _____, Mrs. Lopez always dressed in black.

12. Today is November 25. Christmas is one _____ from today.

13. When he shook my hand, he almost broke it. He doesn't know his own _____.

14. Happy _____ to you! How old are you?

ON YOUR OWN

In your notebook, write sentences with these words.

1. thanks   birthday   _Thanks for the birthday gift._
2. thin   thighs
3. think   bath
4. both   thieves
5. theater   filthy

She'll Be Here Shortly (SH)

My mother is coming over.
When will **she** be here?
Very **shortly.** Can you **wash** the **dishes** for me?
Sure!

INSIGHT

Say the dialogue above out loud and listen to the "SH" sound.

We usually write _____ to show the "SH" sound.

Do you see a word with the "SH" sound that has a special spelling?

Write that word here: _____

> TO SPELL THE "SH" SOUND, WE USUALLY WRITE *SH*.
> SOME WORDS WITH THE "SH" SOUND HAVE SPECIAL
> SPELLINGS.

WORDS TO LEARN

Here are a few common *sh* words with special spellings. Copy them into
your notebook, using the Say-Copy-Check exercise.

sure	machine
sugar	special
tissue	national
issue	social

PRONUNCIATION NOTE

If your native language is not English, you may need to watch out for the
difference between *sh* and *ch*. Here are some common words that begin
with *sh* and *ch*. Make sure you can tell them apart.

sheep:

cheap: not expensive

sheet:

cheat: copy answers on a test

shin:

ship:

chin:

chip:

shoe:

chew:

PRACTICE

Fill in the missing words with the "SH" sound at the beginning or the end. Watch out for special spellings. The first one has been done for you.

1. __Wash__ your hands.

2. It's too hot. Let's stand in the _____.

3. When two people meet, they _____ hands.

4. She's only four feet tall. She is very _____.

5. The baby has a bad case of diaper _____.

6. Will you ever _____ off your beard?

7. You'll get an electric _____ if you touch that wire.

8. I hate it when I'm on a bus and people start to _____ and shove.

9. Mitchell went to the hospital because someone _____ him with a handgun.

10. Are you _____ you're right?

11. I take cream and _____ in my coffee.

12. I just sneezed. Do you have an extra _____ I could use?

13. The washing _____ broke down.

14. They're always going to dances and parties. They have an active _____ life.

15. July 4th is a _____ holiday. Everyone in the country gets it off.

WORD GAMES

Scrambled Words

Unscramble these words. All of the words have the "SH" sound, but some have special spellings. The first one has been done for you.

1. H I P S **SHIP**
2. H A R P S _____
3. S H U R _____
4. H O T S _____
5. H U B S _____
6. S H T E E _____
7. H I S E N _____
8. S A C H _____
9. U S E R _____
10. A R S U G _____
11. S I T S U E _____
12. L S O I A C _____
13. C I A L S P E _____
14. L A T I O N N A _____

Days and Months

On job applications, tax forms, letters, and messages, we often need to write the day of the week or the month of the year. Make sure you know how to spell all these words and their abbreviations. Use the Say-Copy-Check exercise to copy them into your notebook. Note: Some months should not be abbreviated.

January: Jan.	July: July	Monday: Mon.
February: Feb.	August: Aug.	Tuesday: Tues.
March: Mar.	September: Sept.	Wednesday: Wed.
April: Apr.	October: Oct.	Thursday: Thurs.
May: May	November: Nov.	Friday: Fri.
June: June	December: Dec.	Saturday: Sat.
		Sunday: Sun.

PRACTICE

1. Fill in the missing letters. Then write the complete word on the line. The first one has been done for you.

   a. J_a_nu_a_ry _January_

   b. F__b_ __ar__ _____

   c. A__g__s__ _____

   d. Se__t__ __ber _____

   e. De__ __mber _____

   f. M__nda__ _____

   g. Tu__ __day _____

   h. We__ __esday _____

   i. T__ __rsday _____

   j. Sa__ __ __day _____

2. Fill in each date. Use abbreviations where possible. The first one has been done for you.

   a. Tax day: _Apr. 15_

   b. Christmas: _____

   c. New Year's Day: _____

   d. Independence Day: _____

   e. Valentine's Day: _____

   f. Halloween: _____

   g. Your birthday: _____

For complete dates, we write the month, the day, a comma (,), and the year.

For example: March 2, 1981
July 16, 1954

Sometimes we write only numbers. For example, March is the third month of the year, so March 2, 1981, would be 3/2/81. July 16, 1954, would be 7/16/54.

MORE PRACTICE
Write the complete form of each date, spelling out the month. Next, write out the number form. The first one has been done for you.

		Complete	**Number**
1.	Mar. 2, 1981	March 2, 1981	3/2/81
2.	Feb. 21, 1960		
3.	Oct. 13, 1985		
4.	Jan. 5, 1978		
5.	Nov. 12, 1953		
6.	Apr. 9, 1984		
7.	Mar. 20, 1957		
8.	Oct. 18, 1981		
9.	Aug. 3, 1983		
10.	Jan. 25, 1954		

Possessive Nouns

Clara and her daughter each have two dogs.
Clara's dogs are small, but her **daughter's** are large.

INSIGHT

What's small? (*Circle one.*)   Clara   Clara's dogs

What's large? (*Circle one.*)   her daughter   her daughter's dogs

Clara's and *daughter's* are both possessive forms. They answer the question "Whose?" Possessives tell us who has or owns something.

To make *Clara* possessive, we just add 's : *Clara's*.

(The punctuation mark ' is called an *apostrophe*.)

To make *daughter* possessive, we just add 's : *daughter's*.

> POSSESSIVES SHOW WHO OWNS SOMETHING.
> TO MAKE A SINGULAR WORD OR NAME
> POSSESSIVE, JUST ADD 's .

SPECIAL NOTE

If the word or name is singular (shows only one thing or person), you can add 's even if it already ends in *s*.

For example: Thomas's book
the boss's orders

PRACTICE

Make a possessive. The first one has been done for you.

1. Clara —→ dog: *Clara's dog*

2. the man —→ house:

3. Roger —→ sister:

4. my instructor —→ office:

5. Dennis —→ books:

6. that girl —→ hair:

7. Mrs. Lewis —→ husband:

A

This boy has a dog.

It's the **boy's** dog.

B

These two boys have a dog.

It's the **boys'** dog.

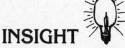

INSIGHT

In Picture A, how many boys are there? _____

There is one boy (singular). Remember that we add ☐ to make the possessive for a singular word.

In Picture B, how many boys are there? _____

There are two boys (plural). To make the possessive for most plural words, we just add ☐.

> TO MAKE MOST PLURAL WORDS POSSESSIVE,
> JUST ADD ☐ TO THE END.

MORE PRACTICE

Make a possessive. The first one has been done for you.

1. the boys ⟶ dog: *the boys' dog*
2. the girls ⟶ teacher: _____
3. the Greens ⟶ house: _____
4. my parents ⟶ money: _____
5. these babies ⟶ mothers: _____
6. the Johnsons ⟶ children: _____

SPECIAL NOTE

Remember that some words have irregular plurals (without -*s*).

For example: man ⟶ men
woman ⟶ women
child ⟶ children

MORE PRACTICE

Since these words do not end in -*s*, we add ☐*s* to make the possessive. Fill in the missing possessives. The first one has been done for you.

1. the people ⟶ dog: **the people's dog**

2. the men ⟶ families: ____

3. the women ⟶ hats: ____

4. the children ⟶ toys: ____

5. the deer ⟶ fawn: ____

SUMMARY OF POSSESSIVES

Add ‎⟦'s⟧ to: all singular words

                irregular plural words that don't end in *-s*

Add ‎⟦'⟧ to: all plural words ending in *-s*

ON YOUR OWN

Practice using possessives on your own.

1. In your notebook, describe your classmates' clothes.

    EXAMPLE: **Larry's** shirt is blue. **Maria's** shoes are gray.

2. In your notebook, describe your relatives' families or friends.

    EXAMPLE: My **sister's** husband is a trucker.

                      My **grandparents'** friends are all over sixty.

CHAPTER 5

Goals

SOUNDS TO SPELL: Different Ways to Spell One Sound
WORDS FOR NOW: Letter to a Teacher
WORDS TO USE: Prepositions
DICTIONARY SKILLS: Trial and Error
Review
WORD PARTS: Suffix Review

WAYS TO SPELL A SOUND

Kind to Call (K)

One reason English spelling can be tricky is that there is more than one way to spell some of the sounds. You're about to learn some of the different ways now. In this lesson, we will learn some of the different ways to make the "K" sound.

Thank you for calling. I'll get **back** to you as soon as I can, and we can **make** an appointment.

When we write the "K" sound at the end of the word, we usually just write the letter __. We write __ __ after a single short vowel. But how do we write the "K" sound at the beginning of a word? Look at these word lists:

SIGHT AND SOUND
Say each word out loud and notice the "K" sound at the beginning.

SAMPLE WORDS

List A	List B	List C
club	call	kind
cry	come	keep
	cut	

INSIGHT

In List A, you see two consonant combos, *cl* and *cr*. Which letter makes the "K" sound in each combo? ____

In List B, what letter shows the "K" sound? ____

Do you see a vowel or a consonant after the *c*? _____

What vowels come after the letter *c*? *a* ____ ____

In List C, what letter shows the "K" sound ____?

Do you see a vowel or consonant after the letter *k*? _____

What vowels do you see after the letter *k*? ____ ____

> ## TO MAKE THE "K" SOUND AT THE BEGINNING OF A WORD, WE USUALLY WRITE *C* BEFORE ANOTHER CONSONANT (IN A COMBO) AND BEFORE THE VOWELS *A, O,* AND *U.* WRITE *K* BEFORE *E* AND *I.*

WORDS TO LEARN
There are only a few words that don't follow the rules. These four words begin with *k* before *a, o,* or *u.* They are exceptions.

karate   kung fu   kangaroo   kayak

PRACTICE
1. Fill in *k* or *c*. The first two have been done for you.

   a. **K**eep

   b. **C**atch

   c. __ey

   d. __ill

   e. __lutch

   f. __an

   g. __iss

   h. __razy

   i. __ult

2. Fill in the missing *c* or *k* words. The first one has been done for you.

   a. I don't **care** anymore.

   b. _____ up the good work.

   c. A baseball hat is called a _____.

   d. Blow out the candles on the birthday _____.

   e. Go fly a _____.

   f. _____ your hands to the music.

   g. _____ the ball with your foot.

   h. Don't _____ the street when the light is red.

   i. What _____ of TV do you have?

   j. That baby is so _____!

3. Fill in the missing words with the "K" sound in the paragraphs below. Some are spelled with the letter *k* and some are spelled with *c*. The first one has been done for you.

   Carolyn is a thirteen-year-old girl who wanted to earn some

money as a baby-sitter. One day she got a phone <u>call</u> from

a

Mrs. White. Mrs. White asked Carolyn to _____ over and take

b

_____ of her baby boy. "Don't worry," said Mrs. White. "My

c

baby's a real good _____. He won't give you any trouble."

d

Carolyn went over, and Mrs. White told her what to do. "If you

take him outside, put on his jacket and put this little _____ on

e

his head. Here is some food for you to _____ for his dinner. I've

f

also left you a _____ of soup to open, and you can have

g

anything else you want. Put the baby to bed at 7:30. Here is the

number where I'll be. Please _____ me if there are any

h

problems."

Everything went fine until Carolyn put on the baby's pajamas

and lifted him into his _____. Right away, the baby started to

i

_____. Carolyn tried singing to him, but he _____ on wailing,

j **k**

and he began to _____ his legs. After twenty minutes, Carolyn

l

was about ready to _____ the baby, but then she thought, "It's

m

not his fault. He's probably scared." She picked him up, and just

then she heard the _____ turn in the lock. Mrs. White was home.

n

"How is my precious baby?" she said, giving him a hug and a

_____. "Was he good?" "Of _____ he was," said Carolyn.

o **p**

There are a few common words with a special spelling of the "K" sound.

SIGHT AND SOUND
Read the words out loud. Say the "K"
sound where you see *ch*.

SAMPLE WORDS
choir   ache

chorus   stomach

INSIGHT
What two letters make the "K" sound in these words? ____ ____

IN SOME WORDS, THE LETTERS *CH* MAKE THE "K" SOUND.

WORDS TO LEARN
Copy the words you need to know into your notebook.

choir   chorus   christen   Christian   Christmas

ache   stomach

WORDS THAT SOUND ALIKE

cord: string or twine
chord: a musical sound

MORE PRACTICE
Fill in the correct word spelled with *ch*. The first one has been done for you.

1. They sang the **chorus** three times.
2. She sings in the church _____.
3. He's got a fat _____ from drinking beer.
4. They put the gifts under the _____ tree.
5. Ow! My fingers _____ from the cold.

Grease on the Dress (S)

The "S" sound has more than one possible spelling.

SIGHT AND SOUND
Say the words out loud. Notice the "S" sound at the end of each word.

SAMPLE WORDS

List A	List B	List C
dress	house	pla_ce)
miss	loose	race
glass	grease	nice

INSIGHT
You have already learned that *ss* (List A) and *se* (List B) at the end of a word make the "S" sound.

List C contains words with a new spelling rule. In List C, which two letters show the "S" sound? ____ ____

Circle the *ce* in each word. Underline the single long vowel that comes before it.

> TO MAKE THE "S" SOUND, WRITE *SS* AFTER A SINGLE SHORT VOWEL. WRITE *SE* AFTER TWO VOWELS TOGETHER (VV). USUALLY WRITE *CE* AFTER A SINGLE LONG VOWEL.

WORDS TO LEARN
Some words have *se* after a single long vowel. Copy them into your notebook using the Say-Copy-Check exercise.

> base   case   chase   vase
>
> dose   close (when it means "near")

Some words with two vowels together (VV) are spelled with *ce*. Learn them.

niece: *niece* and nephew

piece: a part

peace: not war

PRACTICE
1. Fill in *se* or *ce* to make the "S" sound. Then copy the entire word on the line. The first two have been done for you.

   a. grea**se** *grease*   d. lea____ _____

   b. pla**ce** *place*   e. spa____ _____

   c. ni____ _____   f. pri____ _____

g. mou___ _____ **i.** pa___ _____

h. mi___ _____ **j.** spou___ _____

2. Fill in the missing words that end in *ce* or *se*. The first one has been done for you.

   a. Have a ___nice___ day.

   b. To run after: _____

   c. She likes nightgowns with _____ trim.

   d. She wore a blue silk _____ and a blue skirt.

   e. The gambler had a pair of loaded _____.

   f. He disappeared without a _____.

   g. She used a knife to _____ the ham.

   h. Not tight: _____

   i. The ironed fold in your pants legs: _____

   j. Another way to say *near:* _____

   k. Wash your _____ and hands.

   l. They threw _____ at the bride and groom.

SIGHT AND SOUND
Say each word out loud. Listen to the "S" sound at the end of each.

SAMPLE WORDS

List A	List B
el(se)	dan(ce)
course	prince
lapse	chance

INSIGHT

In List A, which two letters show the "S" sound? ___ ___

Do you see a vowel or a consonant before the *se*? _____

Circle the letters *se* and underline the consonants that come before *se*.

In List B, what two letters show the "S" sound? ___ ___

Do you see a vowel or a consonant before *ce*? _____

Circle the letters *ce* and underline the consonant that comes before *ce*. Which letter did you underline? ___

> WE USUALLY WRITE *SE* AFTER A CONSONANT, BUT WE WRITE *CE* AFTER *N*.

WORDS TO LEARN
A few words end in *se* after *n*. Learn them.

dense   sense   tense   rinse

MORE PRACTICE

1. Fill in *se* or *ce*. Then copy the entire word on the line. The first one has been done for you.

   a. cur **se**   **curse**

   b. prin___ _____

   c. pul___ _____

   d. dun___ _____

   e. pur___ _____

   f. min___ _____

   g. wor___ _____

   h. glimp___ _____

2. Fill in the correct *se* and *ce* words. (Watch out for special spellings.) The first one has been done for you.

   a. What **else** do you need today?

   b. She works as a _____ in the hospital.

   c. The doctor put her fingers on my wrist and took my _____.

   d. For better or _____

   e. Do you love me? Of _____ I do.

   f. Dracula lives under an evil _____.

   g. That doesn't make _____.

   h. _____ and princess

   i. There was a barbed wire _____ around the factory.

   j. Every Friday, they go to the disco because they love to _____.

   k. He had the _____ to get a good job, but he passed it up.

   l. The hypnotist put me into a _____.

   m. He took a second _____ at the pretty woman walking down the street.

MORE WORDS TO LEARN

Most short words starting with the "S" sound use the letter *s*. (For example: *see, sit, sand, street*.) A few common words begin with *c* before *e, i,* or *y.*

ceiling   cement   center   cigar   cigarette   circle   circus

citizen   city   cyst   cycle

WORDS THAT SOUND ALIKE

sell: opposite of *buy*
cell: a prison room

sent: past of *send*
cent: a penny

WORD GAMES
Word Grids
Write as many words as you can following the pattern. Words can begin with a single consonant or with a consonant combo. Two words have been filled in for you on the first word grid.

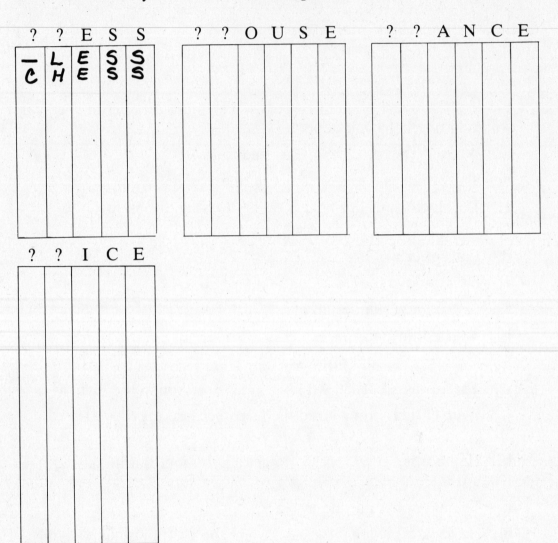

ON YOUR OWN
Write a paragraph about renting a house or an apartment in the city. What are the benefits? What are the problems? When you finish, underline all the words with the "S" sound. (Some useful words are *city, house, lease, price, mice, nice, less, ceiling, fence, chance, close, place, worse, worst.*)

Letter to a Teacher

If you have children, you might need to write notes to their teachers. In these notes, you'd need to explain the children's absences or perhaps talk about a problem the children have been having. As a student yourself, you might need to write a note to your instructor explaining your own absences or problems. Here are some useful words or phrases. Copy the ones you need to know into your notebook.

Dear . . .	doctor	trouble
Sincerely,	dentist	problems
write, writing	appointment	reading
son	hospital	writing
daughter	sick	spelling
because	ill	sore throat
excuse	accident	fever
absent (He was **absent.**)	conference	headache
	please	call
absence (Please excuse his **absence.**)	thank you	contact
	class	concerned
	attend	arrange
	attendance	math
		science
		history

PRACTICE

Fill in the missing words in these letters. Sometimes there is more than one possible correct word. The first one has been done for you.

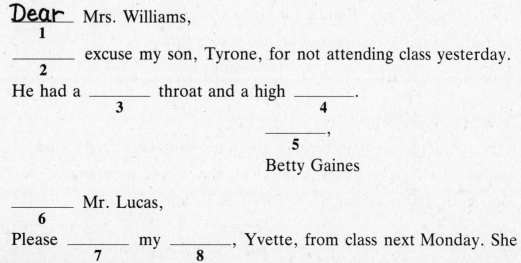

Dear Mrs. Williams,
1

_____ excuse my son, Tyrone, for not attending class yesterday.
2

He had a _____ throat and a high _____.
3 4

_____,
5
Betty Gaines

_____ Mr. Lucas,
6

Please _____ my _____, Yvette, from class next Monday. She
7 8

will be _____ from class _____ I have to take her to the
$\qquad$ 9 $\qquad$ 10

_____ for tests.
11

    Please _____ me at 555-6103 if you have any questions.
12

_____ you.
13

Sincerely,

Marvella Robinson

Dear Miss McNally,

I am _____ about my _____, David. He has done well in
14   15

_____ and _____ classes, but he is having _____ with his
16   17   18

_____ class. Can we arrange a _____? _____ contact me at
19   20   21

555-3257. _____ you very much.
22

_____,
23

Osvaldo Gomez

PROOFREAD
Correct the twenty-nine errors in these letters. The first one has been done for you.

~~Dir~~ *Dear* Mrs. Jones,

Plese excuse my daugther, Cynthia, for not being in class yesterday.
She had a fever and a headake.

Sincerly,
Louise Bates

Dear Mr. Dawson,

Please exuse my sun, Randy, for being abscent yesterday. I had to
take him to the docter becase he had a sore throt.

Sincerely,
Howard Ness

Daer Ms. Weinberg,

I am writting becus I am concern about my daughter, Sheila. She
has been having prolems with her math clas. Could we arange a
confrence? Please contac me at 555-1620. Thank you.

Sincerly,
Ruth N. Frazier

Dear Mr. Ritchie,

I was not able to atend class las week cause I had an acciden. I was in the hoptal for three days. Pleas excus my abcence.

Sincerely,

Leon Freeman

ON YOUR OWN

In your notebook, write letters to your instructor or your child's teacher about three of the following situations.

1. Your son was absent on Monday and Tuesday because he had the flu.

2. Your daughter will be absent next Thursday because you have to take her to the dentist.

3. You were absent from class for two days last week because you had an accident at work.

4. You will be absent from class on Friday because your sister is going into the hospital and you have to take care of her children.

5. You are concerned about your child because he or she has been having problems with reading.

Junior Has Germs (J)

That man is a **jazz genius.**

Say the sentence above out loud. Notice the "J" sound in the bold-type words. Which two letters make the "J" sound at the beginning of the word? ____ ____

THE LETTERS *J* AND *G* BOTH MAKE THE "J" SOUND AT THE BEGINNING OF A WORD. *J* IS USED MORE OFTEN IN SHORT WORDS.

WORDS TO LEARN

Here are some common "J" sound words that begin with *g*.

gel

gem

gene

germ

general

genius

gentle

genuine

Here are some common words spelled with *j* that have special spellings.

jeans

jelly

Jewish

juice

junior

jury

PROOFREAD

Find the word that is spelled wrong. Cross it out and write the correct spelling on the line. The first one has been done for you.

1. jam   ~~jem~~   jet   _gem_
2. geans   genius   gentle   _____
3. jury   junior   jerm   _____
4. gym   gel   gerk   _____
5. gudge   genuine   giraffe   _____
6. jelly   juice   jeneral   _____
7. gem   geep   genius   _____

The **judge** went into a **rage** and decided to **charge** the man with contempt of court.

SIGHT AND SOUND
Say the sentence above out loud. Notice the "J" sound at the end of the bold-type words. Then write each word in the correct list.

SAMPLE WORDS

List A	List B	List C
range	huge	lodge
bulge	stage	badge

INSIGHT

In Lists A and B, *ge* comes after a consonant or single **long** vowel and makes the "J" sound.

In List C, what three letters together make the "J" sound? _____

What comes before the *dge*? (*Circle one.*)   a vowel   a consonant

Is it a long vowel or a short vowel? _____

> AT THE END OF THE WORD, WE USUALLY SPELL THE "J" SOUND WITH THE LETTERS *GE*. (*GE* COMES AFTER A CONSONANT OR A SINGLE **LONG** VOWEL.) WRITE *DGE* AFTER A SINGLE **SHORT** VOWEL.

WORDS TO LEARN
These common "J" sound words have more difficult spellings. Use the Say-Copy-Check exercise to copy them into your notebook.

gauge   orange   manage   manager

PRACTICE
Fill in the missing *ge* or *dge* words. The first one has been done for you.

1. The bird flew out of its **cage**_____.
2. I love chocolate _____ ice cream.
3. I'm gaining weight. My stomach is starting to _____.
4. You have to _____ your bets.
5. Have some _____ juice.
6. Cash or _____?
7. He's weird. His ideas are very _____.
8. Do you wear small, medium, or _____?
9. The musicians came back on _____ after the break.
10. This stupid window is stuck. It won't _____ an inch.
11. I _____ allegiance to the flag of the United States of America.
12. Don't hold a _____ against him.

SPECIAL NOTE

If Spanish is your native language, be careful not to confuse the "Y" and "J" sounds. If you correctly pronounce words with these sounds, you will also spell them correctly. Here are some words to watch out for:

jet: a plane   **jam:** like jelly
yet: up to now (I haven't done it *yet*.)   **yam:** a sweet potato

PROOFREAD

Find and correct the fifteen errors in the paragraph below. The first one has been done for you.

Sometimes I wonder if our justice system is really ~~gust~~ *just*. Some people who commit terrible crimes never go to gail. A few times innocent people have been chardged with a crime and put in prison. Here is a story I once heard.

A lady went into a supermarket, and the manajer noticed a big buldge in her pocket. He reached in and pulled out a yar of gelly. He flew into a raje and accused her of stealing. At her trial, she told the juge she was innocent. She said she'd put the jelly into her yacket at home. The gury didn't believe her story. At first she was sentenced to six months in gail, but then the sentence was chanjed to three months. I don't know if this story is true, but I don't think anyone should go to jail for stealing a gar of yam. What do you think?

WORD GAMES
Word Find

Find the seven hidden words with the "J" sound. They go from left to right and top to bottom. None of the words share letters with each other. Circle real words only.

B	G	E	N	E	T	A	P	S
L	L	J	Y	M	G	Y	M	T
A	C	E	A	E	E	D	G	E
R	T	A	J	A	R	B	O	M
G	O	N	C	U	L	R	P	A
E	R	S	X	G	E	L	I	V

I Guess He's Guilty (G)

Go get the **gun** and **give** it to me.

Say the above sentence out loud and notice the "G" sound at the beginning of the bold-type words. We usually use the letter _____ to show the "G" sound.

I guess he's **guilty.**

Say the sentence out loud. In the bold-type words, which two letters make the "G" sound? ____ (Notice that the *u* is silent.)

Which vowels come after *gu*? ____ ____

> TO SPELL THE "G" SOUND, WE USUALLY WRITE *G*.
> BEFORE *E* OR *I*, WE SOMETIMES WRITE *GU*.

WORDS TO LEARN

Here are some common words that begin with *gu*.

guarantee

guard

guess

guest

guide

guilt

guilty

guitar

There are two other words to learn. They begin with *gh*.

ghost

ghetto

PRACTICE

Fill in the missing "G" sound words. Write *g*, *gu*, or *gh*. (The *gu* and *gh* words you'll need are all on the "Words to Learn" list.) The first one has been done for you.

1. Let's **go** to a movie.

2. Let's play a _____ of poker.

3. Look at the beautiful _____ grass.

4. She has a little boy and a little _____.

5. Be my _____.

6. What's the matter? You look like you've seen a _____!

7. He gave her a birthday _____ wrapped in pink paper.

8. I enjoy music. Can you play the _____?

9. Sorry. I _____ I made a mistake.

10. The security _____ ran after the thief.

ON YOUR OWN
In your notebook, write sentences with these words.

1. girl   grow (or grew)

2. glad   get

3. give (or gave)   guests

4. guess   go

5. ghost   grab (or grabbed)

6. guard   guilty

7. guarantee   good

Prepositions

Get **up.** Get **in.** Get **on.** Get **out.**
Look **up.** Look **down.** Look all **around.**

Read the sentences above out loud. The bold-type words are called **prepositions.** Prepositions are used to connect words. Prepositions are common words that you'll need to spell correctly.

Use the Say-Copy-Check exercise to copy these into your notebook.

up	behind	about	to	during
down	between	around	from	before
in	beside	with	for	after
out	across	into	at	until
on	against		by	
above	underneath			
over	next to			
under				
below				

SPECIAL NOTE
These two words are different.

of: sounds like "uv" or "uh" when we speak fast (a lot *of* people, a piece *of* pie)

off: opposite of *on:* Get *off* the bus. Take *off* your hat.

PRACTICE
1. Fill in the missing letters. Then copy the entire word on the line. The first one has been done for you.

a. do **w** n _down_   f. bes_d_ _____

b. undern_ _th _____   g. ag_ _ns_ _____

c. behi_ _ _____   h. du_in_ _____

d. wi_ _ _____   i. af_ _r _____

e. ar_ _n_ _____   j. unt_ _ _____

2. Look at this picture. Write sentences about it in your notebook. Use prepositions.

    EXAMPLE: The typewriter is **on** the desk.

PROOFREAD
There are nineteen errors in this story. Find and correct them. The first one has been done for you.

    I was ~~en~~ **in** the hospital fer two weeks last year. Dureing my stay, I shared a room wif a man whose bed was acros the room form mine. He was a little strange. Every day a nurse came inta the room whit our medicine. The man would take the pill, put it op to his mouth, and then, when the nurse turned aroun, he'd hold a tissue ap to his lips and start to cough. Afther a while, the nurse got suspicious. She stood nex to him and said, "Open your hand!" The man did, and there was the pill. She began to search the room, and she found pills hidden all ove: behin the water pitcher, onder the pillow, betwen the sheets, undur the bed. Form then on, the nurse always watched the man carefully when he took his medicine.

Where's the Wine? (W)

SIGHT AND SOUND

Say the words in each list out loud. Some people say the words in Lists A and B alike. Some people say them differently.

SAMPLE WORDS

List A	List B
(w)ear	(wh)ere
witch	which
wine	whine

INSIGHT

In List A, what is the first letter in each word? ____

Circle the *w* in each word.

In List B, what are the first two letters in each word? ____ ____

Circle the *wh* in each word.

PRONUNCIATION NOTE

Some people say the "W" sound for the letter *w* and the "WH" sound for the letters *wh*. Other people say the "W" sound for both *w* and *wh*. If you pronounce *w* and *wh* alike, you'll need to study carefully the common words that begin with *wh*.

WORDS TO LEARN

Here are some common *wh* words. Use the Say-Copy-Check exercise to copy them into your notebook.

whack	when	whiskey
wharf	while	whisper
what	whip	whistle
wheat	whiskers	why
wheel	white	

WORDS THAT SOUND ALIKE

whale:

wail: to cry

where: *Where* are you?
wear: What should I *wear* to the party?

whine: cry and complain
wine: a drink

witch:

which: *Which* one is right?

whether: if (I don't know *whether* I'll go or not.)
weather: How is the *weather* today?

PRACTICE

1. Fill in the missing *w* and *wh* words. The first one has been done for you.

    a. She lives **with** her mother.

    b. Someone rang the doorbell _____ I was taking a shower.

    c. I'd love to _____ that contest.

    d. It's cruel to _____ your dog.

    e. Which tie should I _____?

    f. Would you like a glass of _____ with your dinner?

    g. _____ are you?

    h. I don't know _____ way to go.

    i. This bike needs a new front _____.

    j. _____ off your feet on the mat.

    k. They got all _____ in the rain.

2. Read each sentence. Circle the correct word. The first one has been done for you.

    a. (Which, Witch) dress do you like best?

    b. Don't (*whine, wine*). You'll get your candy later.

    c. The baby began to (*whale, wail*).

    d. This (*whether, weather*) is terrible.

    e. She looks like an old (*which, witch*).

    f. I have to (*where, wear*) my glasses when I read.

    g. I don't know (*whether, weather*) or not she'll be here.

    h. Do you prefer red or white (*whine, wine*)?

    i. A (*whale, wail*) is a big animal that lives in the sea.

Trial and Error

Suppose you are writing a sentence and you get stuck on one word.

She ate a (*whole, hole*) chicken.

You know that both *whole* and *hole* are real words, but let's say you can't remember which one is correct for the sentence. Your dictionary will help you. This time you'll need to look at *definitions*, that is, the descriptions or explanations of the words.

Let's find both words now. Look them up in your own dictionary, and you'll find something like this:

> **hole** (hōl) n. 1. An opening or gap 2. A hollow place

> **whole** (hōl) adj. 1. not broken; intact 2. containing all parts; complete; entire

By looking at the definitions of *whole* and *hole,* you can easily see which one belongs in the sentence. We want to say that she ate an *entire* chicken, so the correct word is *whole.*

She ate a **whole** chicken.

Now try another one:

He needs to lose some (*wait, weight*).

Look up both words in your dictionary. The definitions in your own dictionary should be similar to these sample definitions:

> **wait** (wāt) v. 1. to remain in anticipation 2. to postpone 3. to attend or serve

> **weight** (wāt) n. a measure of heaviness

We want to say that he needs to lose some *heaviness,* so we would write:

He needs to lose some **weight.**

PRACTICE

Use the definitions in your dictionary to decide which word is correct for each sentence. Circle the word that is correct and then write it on the line. The first one has been done for you.

1. She (blew, blue) out all of the candles. _blew_
2. The rock shattered the (*pain, pane*) of glass. _____
3. He drove a (*stake, steak*) through the vampire's heart. _____
4. The sky was (*pail, pale*) blue. _____
5. Should I (*mail, male*) this letter now? _____
6. I'm so mad at Bill I could (*ring, wring*) his neck! _____

7. She bought a brand-(*knew*, *new*) car. _____

8. The pots and pans were made of (*steal*, *steel*). _____

9. She plans to (*dye*, *die*) her hair pink. _____

10. The floorboards (*creak*, *creek*) in this old house. _____

11. Separate the egg (*yoke*, *yolk*) from the white. _____

12. He is a (*vial*, *vile*), disgusting man. _____

13. The priest performed the last (*rights*, *rites*) on the dying woman. _____

Review

You've learned all the basic dictionary skills you'll need for good spelling. Let's review these skills now.

> ## WORDS APPEAR IN THE DICTIONARY IN ALPHABETICAL ORDER.

PRACTICE

1. Alphabetize these words as fast as you can. Write the words in your notebook.

   a. break   slip   knit   yellow   whistle

   b. scar   scorn   scare   scab   score

   c. blend   brew   bald   bail   bone   black   brain

> ## GUIDE WORDS AT THE TOP OF EACH DICTIONARY PAGE TELL YOU THE WORDS THAT COME FIRST AND LAST ON EACH PAGE. USE THE GUIDE WORDS TO SPEED YOUR WORD SEARCH.

2. Circle the right guide words for each word. The first one has been done for you.

   a. knuckle   king/knickknack   (knife/Korea)

   b. strand   story/strange   stranger/strenuous

   c. diaper   diameter/diction   dictionary/difficult

   d. alibi   algebra/alias   Algeria/alive

   e. munch   mulch/mummy   mumps/musical

   f. rule   rubbery/rum   Rumania/run

   g. vault   vapor/varsity   vary/vegetable

3. Use your dictionary and the spelling rules you've learned to circle the correct spelling in each sentence. The first one has been done for you.

   a. One and one make (*too, tow,* (*two*)).

   b. I have to (*sale, sell, sill*) my car.

   c. He doesn't know his own (*strenth, strenght, strength*).

   d. Millions (*starf, starve, starv*) every year.

   e. He told the children a long (*tale, tail, tell*).

   f. Subway (*fare, far, fair*) is 75¢.

   g. He came down with the (*flew, flu, floo*) and had to stay home.

   h. As a child, I liked to (*scrall, scrawl, scraul*) all over my books.

   i. I like to (*brows, brouse, browse*) through books in the library.

   j. She (*thought, though, through*) he was handsome.

   k. He has a (*slite, slight, slit*) headache.

   l. He got down on one (*knee, gnee, nee*).

   m. My (*nice, neice, niece*) and nephew just came for a visit.

   n. He ate a (*peace, piece, pease*) of candy.

   o. She wrote a short (*poem, pome, poim*).

   p. They are (*strick, strict, strit*) parents.

   q. Please be (*quit, quiet, quite*).

   r. What does this word (*mean, meen, mind*)?

   s. Lower your voice. There's no need to (*shoot, shout, shut*).

   t. They (*seem, seam, sim*) pleased with their grades.

   u. After his accident, he lost all the (*felling, filling, feeling*) in his left foot.

Suffix Review

-S, -ED, -ING: A REVIEW
We often need to add -s, -ed, and -ing to words. Review the rules now.

-S
• Add -s to most words.
• Add -es to words ending in s, z, ch, sh, and x.
• If a word ends in y after a consonant, change y to i and add -es.

-ED
• Add -ed to most words.
• Add -d to words that already end in e.
• If the word has one vowel and one consonant, double the consonant and add -ed. (Do not double w or x.)
• If the word ends in y after a consonant, change y to i and add -ed.

-ING
• Add -ing to most words.
• If the word has one vowel and one consonant, double the consonant and add -ing. (Do not double w or x.)
• If the word ends in e, drop the e and add -ing.

PRACTICE
1. Add the -s, -ed, or -ing ending to each word. The first three have been done for you.

		-S	-Ed	-Ing
a.	play	plays	played	playing
b.	marry	marries	married	marrying
c.	stop	stops	stopped	stopping
d.	skid			
e.	rake			
f.	clamp			
g.	carry			
h.	stray			
i.	punch			
j.	wrap			
k.	cry			
l.	obey			
m.	press			

2. Change the bold-type word to the correct form by adding -s, -ed, or -ing. Use your notebook. The first one has been done for you.
   a. Right now, I am **write** the answer. <u>Right now, I am writing the answer.</u>
   b. Oh, no. I just **rip** my pants!
   c. My boss **check** my work every day.
   d. Right now, I am **study** spelling.
   e. Susan **wreck** her car last month.
   f. That guy **pitch** so well that he should be a professional ball player.
   g. At this moment, the students are **take** a test.
   h. I **try** to call you yesterday.
   i. She enjoys **put** on perfume.

3. Make these words plural by adding -s or -es. The first one has been done for you.
   a. dress **dresses** _____
   b. block _____
   c. note _____
   d. bat _____
   e. bunch _____
   f. fly _____
   g. tray _____

   ## PROOFREAD
   Check the words with -s, -ed, and -ing endings in the paragraphs below. There are seventeen errors to correct. The first one has been done for you.

       This is Rose's vacation fantasy. She always ~~dreames~~ <u>dreams</u> of fliing to Hawaii for a month. In her mind, she sees milees of golden beachs and rowes of palm trees near the bright blue water. She thinkes about swiming in the warm ocean, plaing on the beach, and just sunbatheing for hours. She knowes that her budget may never allow her to go there, though, so she trys to be happy with shorter trips.

       Last fall, after saveing money for months, she went to Michigan for a week. She and her friend staied in a cabin near a lake. One day, they went fishhing and cookked up everything they caught. Another day, they drove to an orchard and pickked apples. The last night they decided to splurge and go to a nice restaurant. They siped Margaritas and danced until dawn. When she got back, she thought, "It was fun even if it wasn't Hawaii."

Final Words

You've reached the end of the book. By now, English spelling should make a little more sense to you. Let's go over the steps to good spelling:

1. Keep in mind the spelling rules you've learned. They will help you to spell hundreds of words.

2. Pay attention to the way words are spelled. When you see a word whose spelling you want to remember, use the Say-Copy-Check exercise to write the word in your notebook.

3. When in doubt, use your dictionary!

Let's pull it all together now and do some final exercises that review everything you've studied.

PRACTICE 1
Circle the correct spelling.

You (*take   tak   taik*) your education seriously and that is why

1

you are (*devoteing   devoting   devotting*) this time to improving

2

your spelling skills. Good spelling, reading, and

(*writeing   writting   writing*) will help you to (*fine   fin   find*) a

3　　　　　　　　　　　　　　　　　　　　　　　　4

better job and a better life.

It's never (*to   too   two*) late for (*hop   hope   hoped*). A

5　　　　　　　　　　　　　6

person should always hold fast to his or her

(*dreem   dreame   dream*). Even if you (*dropt   droped   dropped*)

7　　　　　　　　　　　　　　　　　　　8

out of (*skool   scool   school*) years ago, you can (*picke   pick   pik*)

9　　　　　　　　　　　　　　　　　　　　　　　10

up where you (*lef   leff   left*) off and keep on improving.

11

Of course it (*migth   might   mite*) not be easy. If you

12

(*want   wont   wannt*) to gain better skills, you have to give

13

(*bothe   bof   both*) time and energy to this effort. Someone who

14

(*tries   tryes   trys*) hard will be able to do it.

15

By finishing this book, you have (*maid   mad   made*) a

16

(_grate great grait_) step. But don't (_quite quit kwit_) now! You
                 17   **18**
are (_readdy reddy ready_) for the (_nex next nexx_) step in your
                  19   **20**
education. Good (_luk lock luck_) to you!
                        21

PRACTICE 2

Add suffixes to each word below. Make other changes only when necessary. Remember everything you have learned about adding -_ing_, -_s_, and -_ed_ to words ending in _y_.

1. play + ed = _____
2. cry + s = _____
3. try + ing = _____
4. stay + ed = _____
5. fly + s = _____
6. spy + ing = _____

7. pay + ing = _____
8. dry + s = _____
9. fry + ed = _____
10. pray + s = _____
11. study + ing = _____
12. marry + ed = _____

PRACTICE 3

Write out each of the amounts below.

1. 7 _____
2. 13 _____
3. 29 _____
4. 18 _____
5. 32 _____

6. 101 _____
7. 21 _____
8. 19 _____
9. 47 _____
10. 390 _____

WORD GAMES
Word Find

There are seven ē words in the grid below. Find and circle them. They go from left to right and from top to bottom. None of the words share letters with each other. Circle real words only.

W	E	A	K	S	J	F
R	M	E	A	T	U	E
E	T	H	I	E	F	E
A	D	E	A	R	V	L
D	S	T	E	A	L	C

PROOFREAD
Cross out the word that is spelled wrong. Fill in the correct spelling on the line.

1. scrach   bleach   crunch _____
2. cruise   masse   boss _____
3. pitch   peach   cach _____
4. grease   leas   mess _____
5. patche   smooch   stitch _____
6. coach   ritch   fetch _____

PRACTICE 4
Make the following bold-type words possessive.

1. **Roger** sister: _____
2. the **babies** toys: _____
3. the **dog** hair: _____
4. the **Dimwitties** mansion: _____
5. the **policemen** car: _____
6. my **parents** jobs: _____

PRACTICE 5
Fill in the missing words with the "K" sound.

1. Children like to eat ice cream with birthday _____.
2. My little sister sings in the church _____.
3. They are going to _____ my baby in a baptism on Good Friday.
4. He went to the library to borrow a _____ to read.
5. The dog bit her leg and now it ____a_____ with pain.
6. This ring isn't real silver. It's _____.

PRACTICE 6
Fill in the missing words with the "J" sound.

1. A ruby is a _____.
2. The _____ found her guilty.
3. Have you ever tasted chocolate _____ ?
4. My job only pays minimum _____.
5. They love to drink _____ juice.
6. He is really smart. He is almost a _____.

WORD GAMES
Crossword Puzzle
Read the clues and write the words in the correct places in the puzzle.

Across

2. When my grandfather was young, he _____ only Spanish.

3. Something you sweep with

6. Chicago is a big _____.

8. The first word in a letter: _____ John

9. On your _____

11. Chicken noodle _____

13. A winter sport

14. _____ and drink

16. Do you prefer to travel by plane, bus, or _____?

17. He walked right _____ me without looking at me.

Down

1. A big meal

2. _____ cigarettes is a bad habit.

3. A bad child

4. Take _____ your hat.

5. _____ on your jacket.

6. The baby _____ when she is hungry.

7. The color of the sun

8. I like potato chips with French onion _____.

10. As a high school student, I couldn't see the blackboard. I went to the eye doctor, and he told me that I _____ glasses.

12. The police found a finger_____ on the gun.

19. The mechanic _____ my car last week. He did a good job.

21. Something a fish has

22. A bird lives in this.

24. I enjoy _____ at the beach.

27. Hey! _____ for me.

28. Hi. _____ are you?

29. Marijuana

30. From beginning to _____

31. Don't play in the _____.

33. What you do to your nails or hair

34. Salt _____ pepper

35. I need _____ pen.

36. Play a guitar

37. He is sitting _____ to his girlfriend.

38. Wash the _____.

40. _____ you very much.

41. He _____ three pieces of pizza last night.

43. He's _____ short to play basketball.

44. You need this to make bread.

46. What happens to your car on a slippery road

47. He has a sore _____.

48. Do you know how to _____ a computer?

13. He has no home. He lives on the _____.

15. Abbreviation for advertisement

18. _____ out your gum!

19. I looked everywhere, but I couldn't _____ it.

20. This and _____

21. Same as 19 down

23. Hey! What are you doing here? I _____ you were out of town.

24. His wheels started to _____ in the mud.

25. One woman, two _____

26. One man, two _____

27. You wear your watch on your _____.

32. Where is the car? I don't remember where I parked _____.

34. She is _____ school.

35. She _____ me a question after the meeting yesterday.

38. Not light

39. Not west

40. I went _____ the store.

42. Don't get mad at me. You know I like to _____ you.

44. I love _____.

45. Same as 41 across

Symbols Used in This Book

SHORT VOWELS
ă: cat

ě: bed

ĭ: sick

ŏ: lock

ŭ: cup

LONG VOWELS
ā: say

ē: be

ī: kite

ō: hope

ū: room, few

SHORT VOWEL PATTERNS
VC: on, hug, drop, split

VCC: ash, sock, drink

LONG VOWEL PATTERNS
VCe: ate, hope, strike

VV: boot, feed, meat, rain

CONSONANTS
The symbols for most consonants are the same as the letters. In some cases, however, there is more than one way to spell a sound. Here are the symbols for sounds with more than one spelling and for special consonants.

G: gas, guilty, ghost

J: jar, page

K: can, key, luck

W or WH: where

CH: check, catch

SH: she, sure

TH: think

S: slice, house, pass

ANSWER KEY

Short Vowel Sounds— pages 5–6

PRACTICE

1. **b.** rest   **g.** else
    c. still   **h.** interest
    d. job   **i.** opposite
    e. upper   **j.** umbrella
    f. add

2. **b.** cut hunk   **g.** lobby rob
    c. ill interest **h.** until rust
    d. bottle olive **i.** ask antenna
    e. upper us   **j.** sick sink
    f. bed rest

MORE PRACTICE

2. hand—*VCC*
3. rob—*VC*
4. less—*VCC*
5. rat—*VC*
6. us—*VC*
7. ill—*VCC*
8. king—*VCC*
9. cap—*VC*
10. cost—*VCC*

Short Vowels and Suffixes—pages 7–8

PRACTICE

2. risks   8. fizzes
3. hisses   9. flashes
4. paths   10. watches
5. rushes   11. dresses
6. bosses   12. rests
7. rafts

MORE PRACTICE

3. asked   asking
4. risked   risking
5. skipped   skipping
6. pressed   pressing
7. wrapped   wrapping
8. trusted   trusting
9. checked   checking
10. burned   burning
11. jumped   jumping
12. rested   resting
13. batted   batting
14. chipped chipping
15. rapped   rapping

Alphabetizing—pages 9–10

PRACTICE

1. **c.** also   steak
        beast   supper
        dictionary   **d.** that
        hate   then
        steal   this
        weird   time
    d. bread   to
        crate   try
        finger   **3.** basic
        letter   letter
        speed   look
        usually   second
2. **b.** see   start
        social   still
        speak

Filling Out a Job Application—pages 11–13

PROOFREAD

FIRM: Betty's Cards and Gifts
ADDRESS: 321 Main St.
DATES WORKED:
FROM 7/82 **TO** present
POSITION HELD: Salesperson
DESCRIBE THE WORK YOU DID:
Sold gifts, worked as a cashier, answered the phone
REASON FOR LEAVING: I'm still working there, but I wish to find a job with more opportunities for advancement.

FIRM: Yummy Burgers Restaurant
ADDRESS: 1517 E. River Rd.
DATES WORKED:
FROM 6/79 **TO** 5/82
POSITION HELD: Waiter
DESCRIBE THE WORK YOU DID:
Helped cook, worked cash register, waited on tables, wrapped food for carryout
REASON FOR LEAVING: The restaurant closed down.

FIRM: Denton's Machine Parts
ADDRESS: 2700 Industrial Rd.
DATES WORKED:
FROM 2/73 **TO** 3/79
POSITION HELD: Shipping clerk
DESCRIBE THE WORK YOU DID:
Filled orders, checked shipments, loaded boxes
REASON FOR LEAVING: I was laid off.

Mop or Mope (VCe)— pages 14–16

PRACTICE

1. b. lake
   c. time
   d. tune
   e. vote

2. b. name
   c. bite
   d. tone
   e. rude
   f. joke
   g. ride

3. Check to see if you got **some** of these words. (You didn't have to get all of them.)
   b. tape—cape, gape, nape, rape
   c. dime—lime, mime, time
   d. nude—dude, rude

PROOFREAD

Dear Laura,

I decided it was ~~tim~~ *time* to send you a little ~~not~~ *note*. I ~~hop~~ *hope* you are well. Not much is new with me. Everything is about the ~~sam~~ *same*. The kids and I are ~~fin~~ *fine*. Oh yes! David won first ~~priz~~ *prize* in an art contest, so we are proud of him.

I still ~~lik~~ *like* my job, but I ~~hat~~ *hate* getting up so early. You know I have to get up at ~~fiv~~ *five* o'clock to get to work on ~~tim~~ *time*. There's only one bus I can ~~tak~~ *take*. Maybe I can ~~sav~~ *save* enough money to get a car. ~~Writ~~ *Write* soon.

Love,
Patricia

Suffixes on VCe Words (-S and -Ed)—page 17

PRACTICE

1. b. bakes, baked
   c. votes, voted
   d. files, filed
   e. rules, ruled
   f. fades, faded
2. Answers will vary.

Suffixes on VCe Words (-Ing)—page 18

PRACTICE

1. b. voting
   c. writing
   d. trading
   e. hoping
   f. making
   g. sliding
   h. joking
   i. shaking
   j. tiling

2. b. hiding
   c. making OR baking
   d. biting
   e. shining
   f. smoking
   g. taking OR writing
   h. wiping

Sweet Dreams (VV)— page 19

PRACTICE

Train Resc(ue)

Thr(ee) girls, all eleven y(ea)rs old, were discovered locked in a tr(ai)n car after a 300-mile trip. The r(ai)lr(oa)d man who saved them said that f(ai)nt m(oa)ns coming from the tr(ai)n car led him to the children.

The girls had climbed in the tr(ai)n car, which was filled with a shipment of b(ee)r, and had hidden in betw(ee)n the packing crates. "It was OK at first," one girl told reporters. "But then we started to f(ee)l hungry and afr(ai)d. We were sure we were going to d(ie)."

The girls wanted to get off the tr(ai)n but had to st(ay) on for 300 miles. There was nothing else to (ea)t, so they had to have b(ee)r to k(ee)p alive. "I never want to see another can of b(ee)r as long as I live," said another girl.

More Suffixes with Long Vowels—page 20

PRACTICE

2. dreams, dreamed, dreaming
3. rains, rained, raining
4. floats, floated, floating
5. prays, prayed, praying
6. shields, shielded, shielding
7. cheats, cheated, cheating
8. loads, loaded, loading
9. beeps, beeped, beeping
10. reaches, reached, reaching
11. mails, mailed, mailing

Suffixes: Double Consonants—pages 21–22

PRACTICE

1. b. taped, taping—VCe
   c. dreamed, dreaming—VV
   d. walked, walking—VCC
   e. leaked, leaking—VV
   f. gripped, gripping—VC
   g. blamed, blaming—VCe
   h. wanted, wanting—VCC
   i. needed, needing—VV
   j. rubbed, rubbing—VC
   k. tricked, tricking—VCC
   l. coped, coping—VCe
   m. choked, choking—VCe
   n. slammed, slamming—VC

2. c. reading
   d. running
   e. making
   f. driving
   g. dealing
   h. playing
   i. waking
   j. getting

PROOFREAD

It's Sunday morning. As I'm ~~wakking~~ *waking* up, I hear the children ~~talkking~~ *talking* and ~~geting~~ *getting* out of bed. I know I should get up too, but I love ~~sleepping~~ *sleeping* late. "Five more minutes," I tell myself. Now the children are ~~runing~~ *running* to the kitchen and ~~makeing~~ *making* breakfast. I can hear them ~~takeing~~ *taking* out the dishes and ~~droping~~ *dropping* some on the floor, but still I don't get up. Now they're ~~pourring~~ *pouring* cereal and milk into their bowls. Soon I hear them ~~eatting~~ *eating*.

"One more minute," I say to myself. Now I can hear them washing the dishes and ~~puting~~ *putting* them away. "What good kids!" I think. But what's that sound? Drip, drip, drip. They've left the faucet on, and water is ~~driping~~ *dripping* into the sink. Drip, drip, drip. It's ~~driveing~~ *driving* me crazy! I can't stand it anymore. I jump out of bed and run to turn off the water. The children are ~~siting~~ *sitting* there and ~~smileing~~ *smiling* at me.

"Good morning!" they say.

Phone Messages—pages 23–24

PRACTICE

2. returned
3. called
4. wants
5. between
6. wants
7. call
8. possible
9. ext.
10. called
11. back
12. before

Mom,
~~Your~~ Your boss ~~call~~ called at 10:00 this ~~mornin.~~ morning
Call him ~~bak.~~ back 555-4234.

Frankie

Elizabeth,
~~Coll~~ Call Gerald ~~tenit~~ tonight ~~befor~~ before 8:30. ~~Irgent.~~ Urgent.

R. Hobbes

Mrs. Johnson,
Mr. Ryan ~~return you~~ returned your call. ~~Pleas~~ Please call
him ~~betwen~~ between 2:00 and 4:00 this
afternoon.

R. Hobbes

Mr. Wolek,
Call Darlene Freeman as ~~son~~ soon as
~~posible. Ligent.~~ possible Urgent 555-1221 ~~etx:~~ ext. 513.

P. Jarvis

Guide Words—pages 25–26
PRACTICE
1. Answers vary depending on your dictionary.
2. b. coil/cola
   c. become/bedlam
   d. rabbit/rail
   e. loaf/log
   f. hose/how
   g. hole/hoop
   h. drill/drop
   i. plane/please
   j. deliver/deserves

Cheers! A Toast! (ō)— pages 27–31
PRACTICE
2. robe
3. boat
4. most
5. host
6. hole
7. coat
8. loan
9. home
10. toe
11. goes
12. roach
13. bone
14. hoe
15. toast
16. goal
17. joke

MORE PRACTICE
1. b. low
   c. slow
   d. show
2. b. old
   c. hold
3. b. owe
   c. bowl
   d. bolt
   e. know
   f. own

b. soap
c. bone
d. bowl
e. roast
f. grow
g. hole

MORE PRACTICE
2. soap
3. cold
4. go
5. home
6. robe
7. toast
8. grow
9. old
10. know
11. don't

A Close Shave (ā)— pages 32–34
PRACTICE
2. made
3. spray paint
4. main, stay
5. page
6. maid
7. plane
8. pray
9. blame

MORE PRACTICE
2. eight
3. waste
4. break
5. steak
6. great
7. weigh
8. waist
9. brake
10. weight
11. change

PROOFREAD
2. nail
3. save
4. raid
5. place
6. taste
7. train
8. change

Looking up a Spelling— pages 35–36
PRACTICE
1. hate
2. caught
3. stale
4. soak
5. dread
6. lurk
7. goal
8. raid
9. slurp

A Fight! A Fight! (ī)— pages 37–39
PRACTICE
2. by
3. cry
4. wide
5. fry
6. wife
7. Tie
8. buy
9. pie
10. mile

MORE PRACTICE
2. kind
3. light
4. might
5. blind
6. night
7. child
8. high
9. height
10. right

PROOFREAD
2. fine
3. child
4. night
5. blind
6. sight
7. bright

Suffixes after Y—pages 40–41
PRACTICE
2. playing
3. crying
4. trying
5. marrying
6. studying

MORE PRACTICE
2. stays, stayed
3. prays, prayed
4. sprays, sprayed
5. strays, strayed
6. obeys, obeyed

MORE PRACTICE
1. b. tries
   c. flies
   d. applies
   e. marries
2. b. fried
   c. spied
   d. dried
   e. studied

MORE PRACTICE
3. trying
4. stayed
5. flies
6. spying
7. paying
8. dries
9. fried
10. prays
11. studying
12. married

Numbers—pages 42–44
1. b. four
   c. thirteen
   d. two
   e. fifteen
   f. nineteen
   g. twenty
   h. twenty-eight
   i. thirty-five
   j. fifty-three
2. b. Twenty
   c. Forty-three
   d. Twelve
   e. Thirty-two
   f. Two hundred

Am I Blue? (ū or o͞o)— pages 45–48
PRACTICE
2. food
3. you
4. room
5. lose
6. prove
7. pool
8. cool
9. mood
10. shoe
11. shoot
12. group
13. through
14. too

MORE PRACTICE
1. b. use
   c. cute
   d. flute
   e. fuse
   f. rule
2. b. stew
   c. true
   d. few
   e. grew
   f. cue
   g. blue
   h. knew
3. b. suit
   c. juice
   d. bruise
   e. beautiful
   f. view
   g. fruit

Where's the Beef? (ē)— pages 49–53
PRACTICE
2. bee
3. speed
4. tree
5. feed
6. feel
7. need
8. week

MORE PRACTICE

2. tea	8. seat
3. beach	9. heat
4. speak	10. rear
5. Clean	11. real
6. teach	12. steal
7. least	13. mean

MORE PRACTICE

2. week	7. weak
3. meat	8. meet
4. hear	9. beat
5. heel	10. here
6. seem	11. heal

PROOFREAD

When I first came to this town, I didn't know anyone. I used to ~~fel~~ *feel* so lonely. I would ~~aet~~ *eat* my ~~meels~~ *meals* alone and ~~reed~~ *read* the newspaper because I had no one to ~~speck~~ *speak* to. Every ~~weak~~ *weak*, I would go out and ~~sea~~ *see* a movie because I had to do something with my ~~fre~~ *free* time. Of course, I wanted to ~~meat~~ *meet* some new ~~peple~~ *people*, but I didn't know how. Then one day on the bus, I started to go to ~~slep~~ *sleep*. Suddenly I thought someone was trying to ~~stael~~ *steal* my umbrella. I opened my eyes and saw a young woman with her hand on my umbrella. "That belongs to ~~mi~~ *me*!" I said. She said, "I'm sorry. I thought it was mine. I'm not a ~~theif~~ *thief*, you know. ~~Hear~~ *Here* is your umbrella." We began to talk, and that's how I met my first ~~reel~~ *real* friend.

WORD GAMES
Crossword Puzzle

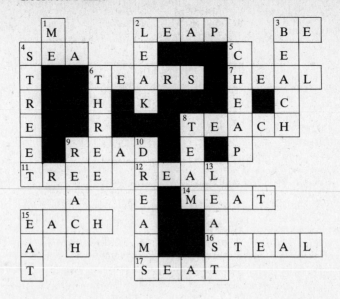

Feel the Chill (ē, ĭ)— pages 54–55
PRACTICE

3. kill	12. fit feet
4. peel	13. hill
5. meal	14. teen
6. sill	15. pill
7. Fill	16. We'll
8. real	17. ship
9. still	18. these
10. steel	19. slip
11. sheep	20. seat

Food Words—pages 56–57
PROOFREAD

1. scrambled eggs
2. pancakes
3. bacon
4. chicken salad sandwich
5. ham sandwich
6. hamburger
7. steak
8. roast turkey
9. mashed potatoes
10. French fries
11. spaghetti
12. soup of the day
13. vegetable of the day
14. fruit salad
15. coffee
16. tea
17. milkshake
18. rice pudding

Snatch a Smooch (CH)—pages 58–59
PRACTICE

2. latch	6. reach
3. couch	7. beach
4. teach	8. clutch
5. stitch	9. slouch

PROOFREAD

2. couch	5. bleach
3. catch	6. crutch
4. teach	7. pitch

Pass the Butter Please (SS/SE)—pages 60–61
PRACTICE

2. pass	6. cross
3. less	7. lease
4. moose	8. dress
5. bruise	

PROOFREAD

2. grease	5. pass
3. choose	6. cheese
4. bless	7. mass

Finding the Right Spelling—pages 62–63
REVIEW PRACTICE

1. a. small think young youth zone
   b. face fact fake fall famous
   c. wad wait want war warm
2. b. kill/king
   c. lift/likelihood
   d. pub/puff
   e. yard/yearn
   f. thong/threw
   g. off/oil

MORE PRACTICE

2. b. mean	g. group
c. team	h. dowel
d. shave	i. freeze
e. slope	j. stain
f. prowl	k. grieve

Plurals—pages 64–68
PRACTICE
4. joints
5. lakes
6. churches
7. spies
8. buses*
9. belts
10. boxes
11. dresses
12. trays
13. bags
14. toys
15. ladies
16. quizzes

*Webster's Dictionary lists *busses* as an acceptable second spelling.

MORE PRACTICE
2. knives
3. shelves
4. leaves
5. halves
6. scarves
7. lives
8. calves
9. loaves
10. thieves

MORE PRACTICE
2. two feet
3. three women
4. one tooth
5. four children
6. two men
7. one mouse
8. three teeth
9. many people
10. one woman

PROOFREAD

I'm one of those ~~person~~ people with a

terrible habit. No, I'm not like those

~~woman~~ Women who smoke and drink or like

those ~~man~~ men who take drugs. What's my

habit? I collect ~~thing~~ things. If you come to

my house, you'll see three or four ~~pile~~ piles

of ~~book~~ books stacked by the door. Then, if

you look inside my closet, you'll see

about ten ~~coat~~ coats and about twenty old

~~shoe~~ shoes and ~~sandal~~ sandals. My living room is

only about ten ~~foot~~ feet long, but it has

two ~~couch~~ couches and five ~~chair~~ chairs. My coffee

table has at least three ~~ashtray~~ ashtrays for all

my ~~guest~~ guests who smoke and also two

~~lamp~~ lamps so there'll be enough light.

Look at one wall, and you'll see thirty

or more ~~photo~~ photos of all my baseball ~~hero~~ heroes,

like Pete Rose, Hank Aaron, and

Roberto Clemente. Look at another

wall and you'll see many ~~postcard~~ postcards of

all the ~~city~~ cities I've ever visited, like New

York, L.A., and Chicago. Walk into

my kitchen, and you'll see I collect

food. On all the ~~shelf~~ shelves of my

refrigerator, you'll find ~~jar~~ jars of ~~leftover~~ leftovers.

I don't always eat them, but I can't

throw them away until they start to

turn green. As you can tell, I live by

myself. Sometimes I think I'd like to

get married and have a few ~~child~~ children, but

where would I find the space?

Three Months (TH)— pages 69–70
PRACTICE
2. Thank
3. throat
4. think
5. Throw
6. thirsty
7. thought
8. through
9. thick
10. bath
11. death
12. month
13. strength
14. birthday

She'll Be Here Shortly (SH)—pages 71–73
PRACTICE
2. shade
3. shake
4. short
5. rash
6. shave
7. shock
8. push
9. shot
10. sure
11. sugar
12. tissue
13. machine
14. social
15. national

WORD GAMES
Scrambled Words
2. sharp
3. rush
4. shot
5. bush
6. sheet
7. shine
8. cash
9. sure
10. sugar
11. tissue
12. social
13. special
14. national

Days and Months—pages 74–75
PRACTICE
1. b. February
   c. August
   d. September
   e. December
   f. Monday
   g. Tuesday
   h. Wednesday
   i. Thursday
   j. Saturday
2. b. Dec. 25
   c. Jan. 1
   d. July 4
   e. Feb. 14
   f. Oct. 31
   g. ?

MORE PRACTICE
2. February 21, 1960   2/21/60
3. October 13, 1985   10/13/85
4. January 5, 1978   1/5/78
5. November 12, 1953   11/12/53
6. April 9, 1984   4/9/84
7. March 20, 1957   3/20/57
8. October 18, 1981   10/18/81
9. August 3, 1983   8/3/83
10. January 25, 1954   1/25/54

Possessive Nouns— pages 76–78
PRACTICE
2. the man's house
3. Roger's sister
4. my instructor's office
5. Dennis's books
6. that girl's hair
7. Mrs. Lewis's husband

MORE PRACTICE
2. the girls' teacher
3. the Greens' house
4. my parents' money
5. these babies' mothers
6. the Johnsons' children

MORE PRACTICE
2. the men's families
3. the women's hats
4. the children's toys
5. the deer's fawn

Kind to Call (K)—pages 79–82
PRACTICE
1. c. key
   d. kill
   e. clutch
   f. can
   g. kiss
   h. crazy
   i. cult
2. b. Keep
   c. cap
   d. cake
   e. kite
   f. Clap
   g. Kick
   h. cross
   i. kind
   j. cute
3. b. come
   c. care
   d. kid
   e. cap
   f. cook
   g. can
   h. call
   i. crib
   j. cry
   k. kept
   l. kick
   m. kill
   n. key
   o. kiss
   p. course

MORE PRACTICE
2. choir
3. stomach
4. Christmas
5. ache

Grease on the Dress (S)—pages 83–86
PRACTICE
1. c. nice
   d. lease
   e. space
   f. price
   g. mouse
   h. mice
   i. pace
   j. spouse
2. b. chase
   c. lace
   d. blouse
   e. dice
   f. trace
   g. slice
      OR dice
   h. loose
   i. crease
   j. close
   k. face
   l. rice

MORE PRACTICE
1. b. prince
   c. pulse
   d. dunce
   e. purse

f. mince   g. sense
g. worse   h. Prince
h. glimpse   i. fence
2. b. nurse   j. dance
   c. pulse   k. chance
   d. worse   l. trance
   e. course   m. glance
   f. curse

WORD GAMES
Word Grids

? ? E S S

-	L	E	S	S
C	H	E	S	S
-	M	E	S	S
B	L	E	S	S
D	R	E	S	S
P	R	E	S	S

? ? O U S E

-	D	O	U	S	E
-	H	O	U	S	E
-	L	O	U	S	E
-	M	O	U	S	E
B	L	O	U	S	E
S	P	O	U	S	E

? ? A N C E

-	D	A	N	C	E
-	L	A	N	C	E
C	H	A	N	C	E
P	R	A	N	C	E
T	R	A	N	C	E
G	L	A	N	C	E

? ? I C E

-	D	I	C	E
-	L	I	C	E
-	M	I	C	E
-	N	I	C	E
-	R	I	C	E
-	V	I	C	E
T	W	I	C	E
S	P	I	C	E
S	L	I	C	E

Letter to a Teacher— pages 87–89
PRACTICE
2. Please
3. sore
4. fever
5. Sincerely
6. Dear
7. excuse
8. daughter
9. absent
10. because
11. hospital OR doctor
12. contact OR call
13. Thank
14. concerned
15. son
16. There are many possible correct answers.
17. There are many possible correct answers.
18. trouble OR problems
19. There are many possible correct answers.
20. conference OR meeting
21. Please
22. Thank
23. Sincerely

PROOFREAD

~~Dif~~ **Dear** Mrs. Jones,

~~Plese~~ **Please** excuse my ~~daugther~~ **daughter**, Cynthia,

for not being in class yesterday. She

had a fever and a ~~headake~~ **headache**.

~~Sincerly,~~ **Sincerely**

Louise Bates

Dear Mr. Dawson,

Please ~~exuse~~ **excuse** my ~~sun~~ **son**, Randy, for being

~~absecnt~~ **absent** yesterday. I had to take him

to the ~~docter beease~~ **doctor because** he had a sore

~~throt.~~ **throat**

Sincerely,

Howard Ness

~~Daer~~ **Dear** Ms. Weinberg,

I am ~~writting becus~~ **writing because** I am ~~concern~~ **concerned**

about my daughter, Sheila. She has

been having ~~prolems~~ **problems** with her math

~~clas~~ **class**. Could we ~~arange~~ **arrange** a ~~confrence~~ **conference**?

Please ~~contac~~ **contact** me at 555-1620.

~~Sincerly,~~ **Sincerely**

Ruth N. Frazier

Dear Mr. Ritchie,

I was not able to ~~atend~~ **attend** class ~~las~~ **last** week

~~cause~~ **because** I had an ~~acciden~~ **accident**. I was in the

hospital ~~hoptal~~ for three days. ~~Pleas exus~~ **Please excuse** my

absence ~~abcense~~.

Sincerely,

Leon Freeman

Junior Has Germs (J)— pages 90–92
PROOFREAD
2. jeans OR genes
3. germ
4. jerk
5. judge
6. general
7. jeep

PRACTICE
2. fudge   8. large
3. bulge   9. stage
4. hedge   10. budge
5. orange   11. pledge
6. charge   12. grudge
7. strange

PROOFREAD

Sometimes I wonder if our justice

system is really ~~gust~~ **jail**. Some people

who commit terrible crimes never go

to ~~gail~~ **jail**. A few times innocent people

have been ~~chardged~~ **charged** with a crime and

put in prison. Here is a story I once

heard.

A lady went into a supermarket,

and the ~~manajer~~ **manager** noticed a big ~~buldge~~ **bulge**

in her pocket. He reached in and

pulled out a ~~yar~~ **jar** of ~~gelly~~ **jelly**. He flew into

a ~~raje~~ **rage** and accused her of stealing. At

her trial, she told the ~~juge~~ **judge** she was

innocent. She said she'd put the jelly

into her ~~yacket~~ **jacket** at home. The ~~gury~~ **jury**

didn't believe her story. At first she

was sentenced to six months in ~~gail~~ **jail**,

but then the sentence was ~~chanjed~~ **changed** to

three months. I don't know if this

story is true, but I don't think anyone

should go to jail for stealing a ~~gar~~ **jar** of

~~yam~~ **jam**. What do you think?

WORD GAMES
Word Find

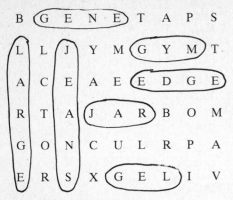

I Guess He's Guilty (G)—pages 93–94
PRACTICE
2. game
3. green
4. girl
5. guest
6. ghost
7. gift
8. guitar
9. guess
10. guard

Prepositions—pages 95–96
PRACTICE
1. b. underneath
   c. behind
   d. with
   e. around
   f. beside
   g. against
   h. during
   i. after
   j. until
2. Here are some sample answers:
   The lamp is **beside** the typewriter.
   The cat is **under** the desk.
   The desk is **between** the chairs.
   The pencil is **in** the desk.
   The TV is **next to** the chair.

PROOFREAD
I was ~~en~~ *in* the hospital ~~fer~~ *for* two weeks last year. ~~Dureing~~ *During* my stay, I shared a room ~~wif~~ *with* a man whose bed was ~~acros~~ *across* the room ~~form~~ *from* mine. He was a little strange. Every day a nurse came ~~inta~~ *into* the room ~~whit~~ *with* our medicine. The man would take the pill, put it ~~op~~ *up* to his mouth, and then, when the nurse turned ~~aroun~~ *around*, he'd hold a tissue ~~ap~~ *up* to his lips and start to cough. ~~Afther~~ *After* a while, the nurse got suspicious. She stood ~~nex~~ *next* to him and

said, "Open your hand!" The man did, and there was the pill. She began to search the room, and she found pills hidden all ~~ove~~ *over* ~~behin~~ *behind* the water pitcher, ~~onder~~ *under* the pillow, ~~betwen~~ *between* the sheets, ~~undur~~ *under* the bed. ~~Form~~ *From* then on, the nurse always watched the man carefully when he took his medicine.

Where's the Wine? (W)—pages 97–98
PRACTICE
1. b. while
   c. win
   d. whip
   e. wear
   f. wine
   g. Where OR Who
   h. which
   i. wheel
   j. Wipe
   k. wet
2. b. whine
   c. wail
   d. weather
   e. witch
   f. wear
   g. whether
   h. wine
   i. whale

Trial and Error—pages 99–100
PRACTICE
2. pane
3. stake
4. pale
5. mail
6. wring
7. new
8. steel
9. dye
10. creak
11. yolk
12. vile
13. rites

Review—pages 101–102
PRACTICE
1. a. break knit slip whistle yellow
   b. scab scar scare score scorn
   c. bail bald black blend bone brain brew
2. b. story/strange
   c. diameter/diction
   d. Algeria/alive
   e. mumps/musical
   f. rubbery/rum
   g. vary/vegetable
3. b. sell
   c. strength
   d. starve
   e. tale
   f. fare
   g. flu
   h. scrawl
   i. browse
   j. thought
   k. slight
   l. knee
   m. niece
   n. piece
   o. poem
   p. strict
   q. quiet
   r. mean
   s. shout
   t. seem
   u. feeling

Suffix Review—pages 103–104
PRACTICE
1. d. skids skidded skidding
   e. rakes raked raking
   f. clamps clamped clamping
   g. carries carried carrying
   h. strays strayed straying
   i. punches punched punching
   j. wraps wrapped wrapping
   k. cries cried crying
   l. obeys obeyed obeying
   m. presses pressed pressing
2. b. Oh, no. I just **ripped** my pants!
   c. My boss **checks** my work every day.
   d. Right now, I am **studying** spelling.
   e. Susan **wrecked** her car last month.
   f. That guy **pitches** so well that he should be a professional ball player.
   g. At this moment, the students are **taking** a test.
   h. I **tried** to call you yesterday.
   i. She enjoys **putting** on perfume.
3. b. blocks
   c. notes
   d. bats
   e. bunches
   f. flies
   g. trays

PROOFREAD
This is Rose's vacation fantasy. She always ~~dreames~~ *dreams* of ~~fliing~~ *flying* to Hawaii for a month. In her mind, she sees ~~milees~~ *miles* of golden ~~beachs~~ *beaches* and ~~rowes~~ *rows* of palm trees near the bright blue water. She ~~thinkes~~ *thinks* about ~~swiming~~ *swimming* in the warm ocean, ~~plaing~~ *playing* on the beach, and just ~~sunbatheing~~ *sunbathing* for hours. She ~~knowes~~ *knows* that her budget may never allow her to go there, though, so she ~~trys~~ *tries* to be happy with shorter trips. Last fall, after ~~saveing~~ *saving* money for months, she went to Michigan for a week. She and her friend ~~staied~~ *stayed* in a cabin near a lake. One day, they went ~~fishhing~~ *fishing* and ~~cookked~~ *cooked* up everything they caught. Another day, they drove to an orchard and ~~pickked~~ *picked* apples. The last night they decided to splurge and go to a nice restaurant. They ~~siped~~ *sipped*

Margaritas and danced until dawn.

When she got back, she thought, "It

was fun even if it wasn't Hawaii."

Final Words—pages 105–109

PRACTICE 1
1. take
2. devoting
3. writing
4. find
5. too
6. hope
7. dream
8. dropped
9. school
10. pick
11. left
12. might
13. want
14. both
15. tries
16. made
17. great
18. quit
19. ready
20. next
21. luck

PRACTICE 2
1. played
2. cries
3. trying
4. stayed
5. flies
6. spying
7. paying
8. dries
9. fried
10. prays
11. studying
12. married

PRACTICE 3
1. seven
2. thirteen
3. twenty-nine
4. eighteen
5. thirty-two
6. one hundred and one
7. twenty-one
8. nineteen
9. forty-seven
10. three hundred and ninety

WORD GAMES
Word Find

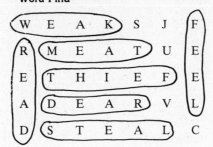

PROOFREAD
1. scratch
2. mass
3. catch
4. lease
5. patch
6. rich

PRACTICE 4
1. Roger's
2. babies'
3. dog's
4. Dimwitties'
5. policemen's
6. parents'

PRACTICE 5
1. cake
2. choir
3. christen
4. book
5. aches
6. fake

PRACTICE 6
1. gem
2. judge
3. fudge
4. wage
5. orange
6. genius

WORD GAMES
Crossword Puzzle